Discovering the Bible

Book Two

Simple Keys for Learning and Praying

Rev. John Tickle

Diocese of El Paso, Texas

LIGUORI PUBLICATIONS

One Liguori Drive
Liguori, Missouri 63057
(314) 464-2500

Imprimi Potest:
Edmund T. Langton, C.SS.R.
Provincial, St. Louis Province
Redemptorist Fathers

Imprimatur:
+ John N. Wurm, S.T.D., Ph.D.
Vicar General, Archdiocese of St. Louis

Cover photo: Tibor Nagy

The illustrations in this book were drawn by Paul DuMond.

Table of Contents

Before You Begin

Like Book One of *Discovering the Bible,* this second book focuses on eight key Biblical themes. By working your way through the Old Testament/New Testament sequence for each theme, you can enter into the world of ancient Hebrew and early Christian experience.

The purpose of this text, however, is not to transport you backward in time. The purpose is to bring the Biblical Word forward into your here-and-now real life. The chapters in this book are specifically geared to help you do this.

The sixteen chapters follow the same simple four-step process. To acquaint yourself with this process, turn to the pages listed as you read the following explanation.

1. *Background section* (see page 7). Work your way through this Background section in whatever way your group will absorb the material best. Some groups prefer the lecture/note-taking method. Others prefer having the participants read the Background section, then raising questions which a trained leader answers or gets the group to answer. (These two approaches can be combined.)

In this initial step the picture on the title page of each chapter can serve as a sort of focal question. For example: *What does this picture bring out that is expressed verbally in the Background material?*

(To insure the most effective use of the Background material found in each chapter, it is recommended that the group leader prepare for each session using the Leader's Guide for *Discovering the Bible — Book Two.*)

2. *Scripture References* (turn to page 8). Have your group go through the Bible, exploring the references given, and writing down their insights *on the theme.* (For this activity, each person will need a copy of the Bible, plus pen and paper.) As the group prefers, either assign a few Scripture references to each person, or have everyone go through all the references. Have each person work privately and silently.

3. *Discussion Questions* (turn to page 9). Using the notes they took while researching the Scripture references, the members should discuss their findings in small groups of three or four persons. After the small-group discussions, the group leader can run through the discussion questions again with the whole group, asking each small group to share their insights with everyone.

4. *Prayer Service* (turn to page 10). This final step brings each session to fulfillment. In this brief experience, your group brings together what took place in their learning/sharing process into a Biblical prayer of praise. (Before you begin each session, select a prayer service leader and a reader for the Scripture reading. Doing this beforehand will give the leader and reader a chance to prepare what they are going to read.)

One of the strengths of this program is its simplicity. With a minimum of planning and preparation, any group from high school upward can learn, share, and *discover the Bible.*

1
Community in the Old Testament

Background

The society of Old Testament times in the ancient Near East revolved around the nomadic clan. A clan was made up of numerous families who were kinfolk to one another. No one in that time would have asked "What is community?" because it was the only form of life they knew. Unity in the clan seemed natural, so that the clan was regarded as one person. Its leader was often, if not always, considered to be the clan himself.

Belonging to the clan was extremely important, especially for security and identity. Society was made up of small villages and cities. Anyone who wandered outside the limits of the town entered a lawless wilderness where he was alone and defenseless. The individual found his total identity within the clan. He accepted the clan's ways and decisions with complete loyalty, for they *were* his own. Literally, to live was to belong to the community.

The ancient Hebrew people lived in this same societal structure. It was the only structure they knew. Their whole mentality was tribal. In Genesis we read how Abraham was called by God — or Yahweh as the Hebrews called God — to "leave your country, your family and your father's house, for the land I will show you." In following Yahweh's call, Abraham takes his clan with him. The blessing for his response is that Yahweh will make a great nation — a great community — out of him, Abraham (Genesis 12:1-3). The fate of the clan-community was completely the fate of the individual within it. There was no difference.

Hebrew community awareness included not only the present members of Israel but stretched back to all ancestors and forward to all descendants. Israelites felt strongly for past, present, and future generations. Not anticipating a life after death, the Israelite saw his immortality in his children and their children for all generations. The community of Israel would thus exist for all time.

There is a folktale about a great Jewish teacher, Honi ha-Meagel, of the first century B.C. When he saw an old man planting a carob tree, he said: "Surely you don't expect to live long enough to see that tree bear fruit? It will take seventy years." The old man replied: "Did I find the world empty when I came into it? Just as my father planted for me, so I am now planting for my children." Jeremiah 29:5-6 expresses a similar sentiment.

The Israelites throughout their history were a special people in the midst of pagan nations. Their calling to be the people of the One True God, to renew the earth, and to be the sign of Yahweh among all peoples made them unique. It also brought suffering and persecution. Their suffering acted as a catalyst to forge even more deeply their sense of community.

The Israelites also recognized a theological importance in their existence as one community. They proclaimed uniquely the revelation that God is ONE and therefore his people are ONE. Their internal unity was itself a sign of the ONE God they worshiped and served.

Exodus chapter 3 recounts one of the greatest moments in Israelite history. Moses is called to free the community of the Israelites. So, Moses goes to Pharaoh and says: "Thus says the Lord, the God of Israel: Let my people go, that they may celebrate a feast to me in the desert" (Exodus 5:1). Together, all Israelites were saved and became free because they were one community before the Lord.

Yahweh proclaimed his faithfulness and love for the community of Israel at Mount Sinai. Leviticus 26:45 recalls that the covenant was between God and his people as a whole. A revered tradition in Judaism is that when the children of Israel stood at the foot of Mount Sinai to receive the covenant, God made them pledge themselves to one another first. From this desire of Yahweh and their obedient reply stem two basic beliefs and traditions of Judaism: All Jews are responsible for each other and all Jews are comrades.

The fourth through the tenth commandments of the Sinai covenant spell out the obligations each individual has to uphold the integrity and unity of the community: Thou shalt not steal, kill, covet, etc. (Exodus 20:1-17; Deuteronomy 5:6-21).

Leviticus 19:2 teaches that the commandments will produce holiness in the community and thus within its members. "The Lord said to Moses, 'Speak to the whole Israelite community and tell them: Be holy, for I, the Lord, your God, am holy.' "

All personal lives were regulated by decisions reached by the community at large. Decisions were made by large numbers or by representatives from clans or families. Seventy persons ratified the covenant with Yahweh for the community (Exodus 24). The people collectively agreed to serve Yahweh under the covenant proclaimed by Joshua (Joshua 24). The elders of the tribes accepted David as king on behalf of the total community (2 Samuel 5).

During the monarchy in Israel, the king was understood to incorporate in himself the entire community of Israel. Thus when David sins with Bathsheba, all of Israel is considered to be sinful (2 Samuel 11). When King David repents (Psalm 51), his personal repentance expresses Israel's desire to receive Yahweh's blessing of forgiveness.

The placing of all community power in the king is also the reason that kings seldom led their armies into battle themselves. A king's death destroyed community vitality.

In the promise to Abraham, in the covenant at Sinai, in the continuation of the community, and in collective decisions, Israel saw the blessing of God. Those blessings from Yahweh were his call to Israel to be a sign for the salvation of the entire world.

In Israelite spirituality, there was simply no thought of the individual having a relationship to Yahweh on his own. Individual identity was part of community identity, and the person's response to Yahweh was part of the community response. This sense of belonging began to change with the work of Jeremiah and Ezekiel around 600 B.C. These great prophets, at much cost to themselves, forged a new stance for the individual before Yahweh. Although still closely tied to the covenant community (reflected in Jeremiah 31:31-34), the individual now bore responsibility for his own obedience or sinfulness. Ezekiel 33:1-20 struggles to express this new idea. These prophets were still closer to community identity than to individual identity. But they took the first Hebrew steps toward a relationship to Yahweh based on individual responsibility.

As Israelites stood at night looking up at the thousands of stars in the desert sky, they could reflect that they were the promised people, the community that would outnumber the stars. They found their identity, their life, their meaning, their faith in blessed membership in the community of Yahweh's chosen ones. Within this community they found security, love, acceptance, and relationship to the Redeemer of Israel, the Creator of the universe. They thanked and praised the Lord!

Scripture References

Yahweh will always remain with the community.
    Isaiah 59:21
    Jeremiah 32:36-41
    Ezekiel 34:25-30

The individual Israelite is blessed because the community "Jerusalem" is blessed.
    Isaiah 65:17-25

The community of Israel saw itself as the source of Yahweh's blessing on all the nations of the earth.
   Psalm 67
   Isaiah 2:2-5

The community of Israel is forgiven by Yahweh as though it were one individual who has returned to Yahweh's love.
   Hosea 14:2-8
   Deuteronomy 28:1-6

Discussion Questions

1. Why was belonging to a community so important for an individual in ancient times?

2. How did the Sinai covenant reflect the nature of the community of Israel?

3. Can the concept of community responsibility for sin or obedience be applied today? If so, how?

4. From what community or communities do I draw my strength?

5. How is my personal faith linked with the faith community to which I belong?

Prayer Service

All: In the name of the Father and of the Son and of the Holy Spirit. Amen.

Leader: Yahweh established his covenant with the community of Israel and now it is written in our hearts. Let us reflect on the words from Scripture that reveal this.

Reader: *(Proclaims Jeremiah 31:31-34.)*

Leader: Let us silently meditate on these words of the Lord.

All: *(Meditate for a few moments.)*

Leader: Let us pray from Psalm 111.

All: The Lord is found in the community of his people.

Leader: I give thanks to Yahweh with all my heart where the virtuous meet and the people assemble. The works of Yahweh are sublime, those who delight in them are right to fix their eyes on them.

All: The Lord is found in the community of his people.

Leader: Every work that he does is full of glory and majesty, and his righteousness can never change. He allows us to commemorate his marvels. Yahweh is merciful and tenderhearted.

All: The Lord is found in the community of his people.

Leader: He provides food for those who fear him; he never forgets his covenant. He reminds his people of the power that he wields by giving them the inheritance of the nations.

All: The Lord is found in the community of his people.

Leader: All that he does is done in faithfulness and justice, in all ways his precepts are dependable.

All: The Lord is found in the community of his people.

Leader: Quickly he comes to his people's rescue, imposing his covenant once and for all; so holy his name, commanding our dread. This fear of Yahweh is the beginning of wisdom, they have sound sense who practice it. His praises will be sung for ever.

All: The Lord is found in the community of his people.

Leader: Let us pray together:

Lord Yahweh, our God, may we never forget the history of your calling us as a people to serve you and be a sign of your love and mercy to all people everywhere. May we always seek ways to come together as a community of your faithful to proclaim your glory and give you praise. We ask this in Jesus' name. Amen.

2
Community in the New Testament

Background

Pentecost is viewed today as the beginning of the Christian community. Although Jesus' followers had doubtless been close, the coming of the Holy Spirit gave them a deeper unity. Acts chapter 2 records how they found the strength and the courage to witness to Jesus. Now the newly Spirit-filled Christian community experienced oneness in the Lord as they spread the message of Jesus' Resurrection.

The earliest community was, of course, Jewish. They were different from other Jews only in that they believed in Jesus as the promised Messiah. They kept up Jewish practices such as the cleanliness laws and Sabbath worship. They continued to think of themselves as members of the Jewish community. They still frequented the Temple to pray, even as they heard the teaching of the apostles (Acts 2:42-47).

As believers in the Messiah, they understood themselves to have experienced the fulfillment of ancient prophecies. The Spirit of Yahweh, promised hundreds of years before, had now been communicated to an entire community of people (compare Acts 2:14-21 with Joel 3:1-5).

They found other parallels between their community experience and the ancient Israelite community. Centuries before, Israel had seen itself to be a community with a saving mission to the whole world. Now the community of Jesus' believers saw themselves in the same way, empowered by the Spirit (1 Peter 2:9-12). The unity of Jesus' followers in the Spirit produced a sense of togetherness that entailed definite responsibilities on the part of each individual.

The older Jewish community had been strengthened by persecution. This was also the case with Jesus' followers. When persecution of the spirited community began, some disciples were forced to leave Jerusalem for other parts of Judea. Their missionary activities were born as they preached Jesus in Samaria and Galilee.

They formed new little communities of believers wherever they preached, centering on the death and Resurrection of Jesus. As Gentiles began to believe in Jesus, too, conflict grew between Jews who did not believe in Jesus and Jews who did. In Antioch, the believers in Jesus first began to be known as Christians. At the time, it was not a compliment. The division between Judaism and Christianity began, but Christians drew closer together.

Through the Holy Spirit, the Christian community came to one of its deepest theological understandings: It was communion with the Lord Jesus that led to their union with one another. Jesus in his very person effected the perfect union between Yahweh and his people (Hebrews 2:14-18, 3:1-6).

This perfect union expressed itself in their love for one another. This is why they pooled their worldly possessions and sought to serve each other with humble dedication (Acts 4:32-33). They would eventually cover the earth with this living message: It is love for one another that builds up the community which is the Body of the Lord Jesus.

Their experience of unity with Jesus and with one another was so intense that it gave birth to a deep new insight: Saint Paul's teaching on the Mystical Body of Christ. Paul's descriptions of this unity and the analogy of the body are found in the following passages: Romans 6:3-11; 2 Corinthians 4:14; Ephesians 2:4-6; Philippians 3:9-11; and 1 Corinthians 12:12-31.

The community of Jesus came, in time, to understand that the Spirit continues to give life to the community through the sacraments. They found the presence of the Lord in Baptism and the Eucharist. Saint John teaches: "Thus there are three that testify, the Spirit and the water and the blood — and these three are of one accord" (1 John 5:7).

Baptism brings each person into the Body of Christ, into a personal union with the community of the faithful. Baptism makes the Christian community (the Church) a living community. It enables each individual to become part of the vine of the Lord (John 15:1-7).

For the early Christians, love was not automatic nor easily found in every experience of the sacraments. In fact, if those in Corinth had not had difficulties, Saint Paul might not have written his clear instructions about the celebration of the Eucharist (1 Corinthians 11:17-34). Nevertheless, Christians came to understand that love within the community flows from participation in the Eucharist. The celebration of the Eucharist was called the "breaking of the bread," recalling the final meal Jesus had celebrated with his family-community the night before his death. In his memory, they gathered in private homes to celebrate the Eucharist. The leader of the gathering would pronounce the same words of thanksgiving that Jesus had said at the Last Supper.

The Christian community increasingly saw itself as separate from the world (John 17:16). They believed that in the community itself one finds the way to eternal life. One even begins to participate in that eternity right now (1 John 2:15-17). As the persecution of the community grew toward the end of the first century, Christians began to use symbols to communicate this faith.

Some of these symbols were common to older Jewish persecution-literature as well. In the imagery of the woman and the dragon in the Book of Revelation, chapter 12, the woman represents both the old Israel and the new Israel — the People of God, the Christian community. The woman gives birth to, and is one with, the Son who is to rule all the nations. She flees into the desert to escape persecution, as did Israel of old in fleeing from Egypt.

The dragon, symbolizing evil, pursues the woman in vain. In verse 17 of chapter 12, the dragon goes off "to make war on the rest of her children, that is, all who obey God's commandments and bear witness for Jesus." John here makes the distinction between the community of the Church, which is represented by the woman, and the individuals in the community. Individuals reach this perfect existence to the extent that they live the community mission of keeping the covenant commandments and giving witness to Jesus.

Much later — after the New Testament writings had been completed — Christians also saw the figure of Mary in the symbol of the woman. They held Mary in reverence as the symbol of the mission and message of the community.

The sense of increasing separation from the world and participation in a loving eternity were strengthened by belief that the return of the Lord was close at hand. As 1 Peter 4:7-11 describes, they lived very closely together, loving and suffering as they awaited his coming. That expectation was not fulfilled in their lifetime, as they hoped. But the Christian community lived on. Now, two thousand years later, the Spirit of Pentecost can still be seen and felt whenever we continue to live as a community of love and service to all.

Scripture References

At Pentecost the Spirit was communicated to the entire community as had been foretold by the prophets.

    Joel 3:1-5
    Acts 2:14-36

The community of Jesus believed its mission was that of the Lord to all the world.

    1 Peter 2:9-12
    Matthew 28:16-20
    John 10:16

Jesus effected the perfect union between God and his people.

    Hebrews 2:14-18
    John 14:6-11, 17:21

Each individual in the Christian community who believes is joined into the Mystical Body of the Lord.

    1 Corinthians 12:12-31
    Romans 6:3-11
    Ephesians 2:4-6

The celebration of the Eucharist unifies and nourishes the community.

    1 Corinthians 11:17-37
    John 6:1-13, 53-58

Discussion Questions

1. What was the significance of the Pentecost experience for the early community of followers of Jesus?

2. What was required of an individual to belong to the community of Jesus?

3. What is meant by saying that the person of Jesus effects the perfect union between God and his people?

4. Do I experience the life of the Spirit in the Eucharist? Why or why not?

5. Do I feel that I am joined to Jesus himself in his community of the faithful? Why or why not?

6. How has my faith increased over the years by responding to life with loving?

7. How can I help form in my family a clearer example of the community of Jesus?

Prayer Service

All: In the name of the Father and of the Son and of the Holy Spirit. Amen.

Leader: Jesus binds us together in his community by his love and commands us to love all people that his saving power might touch the whole world. Let us reflect on the words of Scripture that inspire this need.

Reader: (Proclaims 1 Corinthians 13:1-13.)

Leader: Let us silently meditate on these sacred words.

All: (Meditate for a few moments.)

Leader: Let us respond to these words from Scripture by praying from the letter to the Ephesians (4:1-6).

All: Praise the Lord for making us one people!

Leader: I, the prisoner in the Lord, implore you therefore to lead a life worthy of your vocation.

All: Praise the Lord for making us one people!

Leader: Bear with one another charitably, in complete selflessness, gentleness, and patience.

All: Praise the Lord for making us one people!

Leader: Do all you can to preserve the unity of the Spirit by the peace that binds you together.

All: Praise the Lord for making us one people!

Leader: There is one Body, one Spirit, just as you were all called into one and the same hope when you were called.

All: Praise the Lord for making us one people!

Leader: There is one Lord, one faith, one baptism, and one God who is Father of all, over all, through all, and within all.

All: Praise the Lord for making us one people!

Leader: Let us pray together:
              Jesus, our Lord and Savior, we give you thanks and praise for calling us to be your people. Inspired by your loving example and empowered by the Spirit, may we live our lives sharing love and concern to all within the universal community of your creation. Amen.

3
Hospitality in the Old Testament

Background

Hospitality, in Old Testament times, meant the sharing of food, water, and shelter. It was rooted in the necessity of sharing for survival. This need exists even today among nomadic people in the desert regions of the Middle East. Without hospitality — shelter from heat and animals — wandering desert nomads could die from thirst, hunger, and the dangers of the wilderness.

This basic nomadic necessity is reflected throughout the Old Testament. All the way back to Abraham, hospitality was regarded as one of the primary virtues among the ancient nomadic Hebrews. Abraham, the first patriarch of Israel, gave the example to all succeeding ages of Israelites of the prime importance of the practice of welcoming strangers (Genesis chapter 18). The Hebrews never forgot that these strangers turned out to be divine messengers. Other early examples may be found in Genesis 24:28-32 and Judges 19:16-24.

Hospitality sometimes included a blessing. When Abraham and his allied kings were welcomed by Melchizedek, king of Salem, he brought them bread and wine and pronounced the blessing recorded in Genesis 14:17-20. Abraham responded to his hospitality by giving the king of Salem a tenth of his booty.

The hospitality of a meal bound the participants in a sacred bond. Even if he was an enemy, a guest at table could not be betrayed by the host or anyone in his clan. Thus if they were former enemies, the hospitality shown to the guest was a reconciliation. Just as the host must protect the guest, so the guest must not cause offense to the host. Both were immune from all harm for at least three days. Their presence to one another was sacred. So David invited his potential enemy to his table in order to preclude bloodshed (2 Samuel 9:1-7).

The earliest and most consistent rite of hospitality in the Old Testament was the washing of feet (Genesis 18:1-8, 24:30-32; Tobit 7:1-9) which the host made possible for the guest. Another welcoming gesture was the anointing of the head with oil (Psalm 23:5). When a traveling stranger entered a town and knew no one so that he needed hospitality, he would go and sit in the town square. The townspeople were (at least theoretically) obligated to provide for him (Judges 19:16-24).

The extreme extent to which the virtue of hospitality was sometimes carried is illustrated by the example of Lot. He was willing for the men of Sodom to ravish his daughters rather than turn over his guests to them (Genesis 19:4-11). This seems quite out of order today, but it indicates the value placed on the inviolability of the stranger who was a guest.

Of course, in the desert, water is a primary issue: whose it is and where to find it. Their lives centered around the places where it could be acquired (Genesis 26:14-22). Because of the absolute necessity of water, one of Yahweh's greatest saving blessings on his people was his provision of water. In the desert of Sinai (Exodus 15:22-27, 17:1-7) when Yahweh again saved his people by giving them water, the people easily began to see him as the source of "living" water. He was a host in this way to his people. In Psalm 15 there is a poem describing who is worthy to be guest to Yahweh. Yahweh was praised for all his saving acts, including this kind of hospitality. And so each human act of hospitality was viewed as proclaiming the glory of God.

Even a stronger urge to hospitality was the recognition that the stranger in their midst symbolized Israel's own history as an alien people in Egypt. As they had benefited from the hospitality of others, so now the stranger had definite though limited rights among them. Part of their vocation from Yahweh was the benevolence shown to the stranger, for he represented the "poor" whom Yahweh particularly protected (Leviticus 19:10; Deuteronomy 10:17-19). An excellent example of such protective hospitality is found in Ruth 2:1-10.

Ancient teaching proclaimed that when the poor took part in a meal offered by Yahweh through his people, they were enacting a sign of the final kingdom of Yahweh (Isaiah 55:1-3). Even the acquisition of divine wisdom was symbolized by participation in a meal (Proverbs 9:1-6).

Sacred custom prescribed that at mealtimes all the families of Israel were to set out little flags so that the poor and strangers would know they were welcome to food that was being served. Families were even encouraged to linger at meals so that strangers might have time to find them and be welcomed.

Working through the customs of these nomadic people, Yahweh revealed the importance of sharing in hospitality for one another — for the poor, for strangers, even for enemies. Hospitality became one way to manifest loyalty to the covenant between Yahweh and Israel. The sharing of food reminded all of Yahweh's sharing of life with his people.

Scripture References

Abraham set the patriarchal example of hospitality.
> Genesis 18:1-8

Places where there was water were of prime importance to Israel. Here water was the symbol of Yahweh's saving care for his people.
> Exodus 15:22-27
> 17:1-7

Hospitality was to be shown to the poor and the stranger, for Yahweh protected them.
> Leviticus 19:10
> Deuteronomy 10:17-19

The washing of feet and anointing with oil were special ritual acts of hospitality.
> Tobit 7:9
> Genesis 24:30-32
> Psalm 32:5

Food, drink, and refreshment shared were the signs of the final kingdom of Yahweh.
> Isaiah 55:1-3

Discussion Questions

1. Why was hospitality a primary virtue for nomadic people?

2. In the Book of Exodus, why did the people link Moses' providing of water with Yahweh's covenant promises to his people?

3. What practical privileges did the stranger gain when he became a guest at a meal?

4. How did hospitality become a sign of the vocation of Israel?

5. What blessings and benefits have I experienced from being hospitable in my relationships with others?

6. How can the family meal be a perfect time for practicing the ancient virtue of hospitality?

7. Why do we not share hospitality with the poor and the stranger as our Jewish ancestors did?

Prayer Service

All: In the name of the Father and of the Son and of the Holy Spirit. Amen.

Leader: From the origins of our faith, Abraham teaches us by his example the virtue of hospitality. Let us reflect and be inspired by the account of his action.

Reader: *(Proclaims Genesis 18:1-8.)*

Leader: Let us silently meditate on the words of Scripture we have just heard.

All: *(Meditate for a few moments.)*

Leader: Let us pray from Psalm 23.

All: The Lord is the hospitable Savior!

Leader: Yahweh is my shepherd, I lack nothing. In meadows of green grass he lets me lie. To the waters of repose he leads me; there he revives my soul.

All: The Lord is the hospitable Savior!

Leader: He guides me by paths of virtue for the sake of his name. Though I pass through a gloomy valley, I fear no harm; beside me your rod and your staff are there, to hearten me.

All: The Lord is the hospitable Savior!

Leader: You prepare a table before me under the eyes of my enemies; you anoint my head with oil, my cup brims over.

All: The Lord is the hospitable Savior!

Leader: Ah, how goodness and kindness pursue me, every day of my life; my home, the house of Yahweh, as long as I live!

All: The Lord is the hospitable Savior!

Leader: Let us pray together:

All: Lord God, our Father, your hospitality to us, your people, inspires us to be hospitable to all, especially to the poor and the stranger. Excite within us the desire to practice this virtue daily so that you may be given glory and praise from all the earth. We pray in the name of Jesus through the Holy Spirit. Amen.

4
Hospitality in the New Testament

Background

The leaders and most of the people in the earliest Christian community were Jewish. They kept their Jewish mentality, values, and customs. But they found these things fulfilled in the person and teaching of Jesus.

As in Old Testament times, the early Christians used the washing of feet as a rite of hospitality and service (1 Timothy 5:10). For 2,000 years Christians have remembered the woman who expressed her love for Jesus in this way, while his hosts ignored such service (Luke 7:36-50). Jesus himself used this rite as a symbol of his total self-giving for his followers (John 13:1-15).

As the virtue of hospitality had been primary for their ancestors, so Christians must host others graciously without complaining (1 Peter 4:8-9). Hospitality within the Christian community became a means of practicing their desire to follow the Master's loving way of salvation. Their hospitality to strangers, especially pagans, reciprocated the welcome that Jesus had shown to each one in the community. In the Master's hospitality to his followers, they were enabled to live securely.

Jesus used hospitality as an opportunity to express his love. He, the Lord of Life, brought salvation to those who would welcome him and thus be bound together with him. Zacchaeus participated in this saving love when the Lord chose to receive his hospitality and share his Father's message (Luke 19:1-10). Jesus saw his followers as hosts of God, honored by God's presence as guest. "Anyone who loves me will be true to my word, and my Father will love him; we will come to him and make our dwelling place with him" (John 14:23). Jesus emphasized hospitality when he pictured himself knocking at the door waiting for us to open and receive him. Without our gracious hospitality toward him, he is unable to come and dwell in our midst (Revelation 3:20).

On earth Jesus often felt the lack of hospitality from his own people. The nativity account (Luke 2:7) recalls his birth in a stable because there had been no place in the inns. Luke 9:58 may reflect the Lord's feeling of aloneness, his need for hospitality: "The foxes have lairs, the birds of the sky have nests, but the Son of Man has nowhere to lay his head."

The Lord identified himself totally with those who needed the hospitality of others in order to survive — the hungry, the naked, those in prison, the traveler. The community of his followers would one day be judged as they had or had not offered hospitality to their brothers and thus to Jesus himself (Matthew 25:34-45).

When Jesus first sent out his disciples, he instructed them to depend completely on those who would receive them. The daily needs of their existence were to be met by hospitality (Luke 9:1-6). Later in the early Church, these instructions were followed. The apostles and disciples depended on the hospitality of the Christian communities, which freed them to preach the Good News (Acts 14:28, 15:33). In 3 John 5-8, the writer praises Gaius as the perfect example of Christian hospitality. Hospitality was considered one of the necessary virtues of the earliest bishops in the community (1 Timothy 3:2).

Paul reprimands the community at Corinth for its lack of hospitality when they gathered for Eucharist. "When you assemble it is not to eat the Lord's supper, for everyone is in haste to eat his own supper. One person goes hungry while another gets drunk" (1 Corinthians 12:20-21). The sharing of the one loaf and the one cup of the Eucharist made the community one. It encouraged complete fellowship. In Hebrews 13:1-2, the author reminds the community: "Love your fellow Christians always. Do not neglect to show hospitality, for by that means some have entertained angels without knowing it" — a reference to Abraham in Genesis chapter 18.

Finally, the Christian community would discipline false teachers by refusing them hospitality, cutting them off from the life of the community (2 John 9-11).

The Jewish-Christian understanding of their oneness with Yahweh, with Jesus the Lord, and with all people inspired them to practice concern and care for everyone — especially the poor and strangers. The kingdom would finally come when charity commanded the hearts of all the Lord's followers.

Scripture References

The community of Jesus was to live harmoniously in order to give glory to God.
  Romans 15:1-7

The apostles were sent forth by Jesus dependent on the hospitality of those who heard their message.
  Luke 9:1-6

Jesus identified himself with those in need of hospitality and service.
  Matthew 25:34-45

Jesus is the "living water."
  John 4:4-14

The washing of the feet and anointing with oil demonstrated hospitality, humility, and selfless service of others.
  John 13:1-15
  1 Timothy 5:10
  Luke 7:36-50

Discussion Questions

1. How did hospitality fulfill Jesus' command to love another?

2. How is hospitality related to salvation?

3. Why did Jesus identify himself with the imprisoned, the sick, the naked, and the stranger?

4. What acts of hospitality do I manifest in my daily living as a Christian?

5. Who in my life is in need of my hospitality?

Prayer Service

All: In the name of the Father and of the Son and of the Holy Spirit. Amen.

Leader: Jesus teaches us that love must be practical if it is to bring salvation. Let us reflect on the encouraging words that Paul gives us in his letter to the Romans.

Reader: *(Proclaims Romans 12:9-18.)*

Leader: Let us meditate silently on this Good News.

All: *(Meditate for a few moments.)*

Leader: Let us pray with the words Jesus addressed to his disciples on the night before his Passion and death (John 15).

All: The Lord lives on through our love.

Leader: As the Father has loved me, so I have loved you. Remain in my love.

All: The Lord lives on through our love.

Leader: If you keep my commandments you will remain in my love, just as I have kept my Father's commandments and remain in his love.

All: The Lord lives on through our love.

Leader: You did not choose me, no, I chose you; and I commissioned you to go out and to bear fruit, fruit that will last; and then the Father will give you anything that you ask him in my name.

All: The Lord lives on through our love.

Leader: What I command you is to love one another.

All: The Lord lives on through our love.

Leader: Let us pray together:

All: Lord Jesus, by your example, we are urged to live lives of hospitality toward each other. Through this practice of love, we feel your presence and extend your salvation to all. May we never cease searching for ways to make all feel at home with us and with you. Amen.

5
Faith in the Old Testament

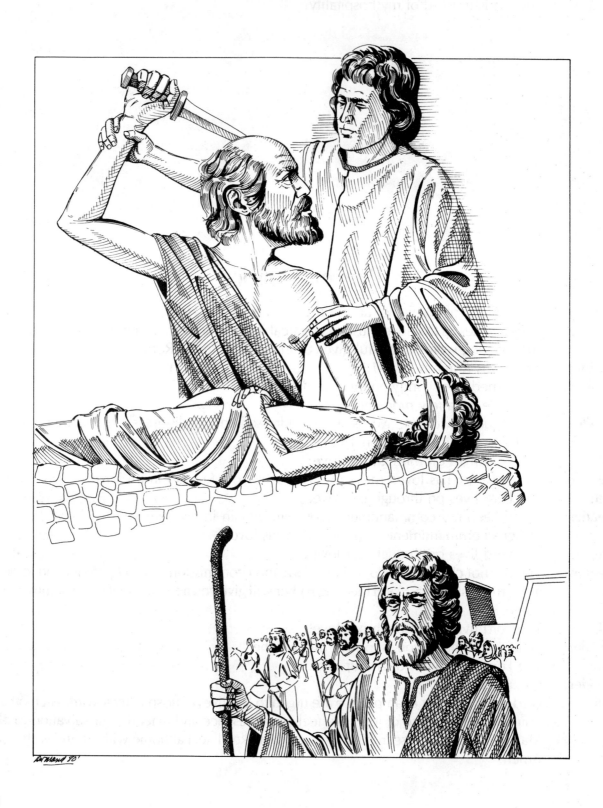

Background

The Hebrew verb for "having faith" is the word 'aman. In its several forms, it always refers in some way to firmness, solidity, security. So, a person who has faith is firm and secure.

Yahweh is called faithful, meaning solid, certain, true, reliable.

The relationship between Israel and Yahweh is faithful, meaning that Israel's firmness and security are based on the certainty and trustworthiness of Yahweh.

Old Testament faith was concrete. It was based firmly on Israel's experience of Yahweh in history. They knew Yahweh controlled their history. This certainty was their faith.

Since God is utterly reliable, Biblical faith means that we can put ourselves entirely in his hands. We can freely recognize our total inability to live without his power. We can be totally confident in his providence and loving kindness. If we remain in this faith, this solidity, we cease to rely on our own resources or on those of other humans. We depend on Yahweh's will for us. To put it in Old Testament terms: since he has done so much for us in our history, we can count on him to keep us secure.

The figure most closely associated with faith in Israelite history is Abraham. He obediently left his home to be led wherever Yahweh wished. Yahweh promised that he would have innumerable descendants (Genesis 12:1-2, 13:14-17, 15:1-6). Abraham put his whole trust in that promise.

The supreme demonstration of Abraham's confidence in Yahweh was his willingness to give Yahweh his son, the bearer of Yahweh's promise. Yahweh clearly rejects this offer of child sacrifice. Yet we can still see here Abraham's complete trust in Yahweh's trustworthiness. Yahweh had promised; Yahweh would keep his promise. The story is recorded in Genesis 22:1-19. Abraham knew that for everything to turn out according to Yahweh's promise, he needed only to remain faithful, to surrender himself and his people to Yahweh.

The event which created the faith of the chosen community was the Exodus to freedom from slavery in Egypt. It was because of this event that Israel knew Yahweh was solid and effective in their life. The community collaborated actively with Yahweh by accepting his covenant agreement. Their own demonstration of faithfulness was to be their obedience within the covenant (Exodus 19:3-8). Keeping covenant faithfully implied confidence in Yahweh, certainty, hope, love, and obedience by the entire community of Israel.

When Israel lost their trust in Yahweh, or forgot what he had done for them, they turned to idolatry and practiced a legalistic, ritualistic religion. When this occurred, the prophets objected strongly (Amos 5:21-25; Isaiah 1:4 and 29:13-16).

Israel had a difficult time remaining faithful. In times of prosperity, it was easy to forget their dependence and adopt an attitude of self-reliance. When they were victorious in a military conflict, they tended to think they had done it all themselves.

They also tended toward the opposite extreme. When they were under serious threat, they thought Yahweh had deserted them. Then they would turn to pagan gods for protection and security. But how could they remain certain of something that was not reliable?

The prophet Jeremiah reminded Israel of their plight: "Thus says the Lord: Cursed is the man who trusts in human beings, who seeks his strength in flesh, whose heart turns away from the Lord" (Jeremiah 17:5-8).

Isaiah of Jerusalem urged dependence on Yahweh instead of on horses (a military weapon) in Isaiah 30:15-16. Psalm 52:8-9 echoes this same theme. In fact, it is to be found throughout the Old Testament.

When Israel's faith so often failed, the prophets proclaimed the healing message of Yahweh: if you repent and turn away from your evil ways toward me, I will return in covenant to you (Ezekiel 33:10-11; Deuteronomy 4:28-31). Jeremiah, looking at the distress and failure of the chosen ones, pleaded that they turn from their ways (Jeremiah 13:15-17). The prophet even turned to Yahweh in confession for his people. Just as they had been unfaithful, Jeremiah knew that Yahweh was somehow active in saving them from all that had befallen them (Jeremiah 14:19-22).

Isaiah proclaimed loud and clear: "Unless your faith is firm, you shall not be firm" (Isaiah 7:9). For the prophets, and ultimately for all Israel, faith was the basis of all blessings and of salvation. Nothing good could come to Israel except from Yahweh through their trust in him (Deuteronomy 28:1-6).

Faithfulness insured life and security for Israel. Revolt and forgetfulness of Yahweh always produced insecurity and lack of unity, and Israel's inability to fulfill its mission. When suffering, death, and calamities came, they always followed on the heels of faithlessness. But when Israel in its pain again sought Yahweh, the prophet spoke comfort from Yahweh (Isaiah 43:1-4). Then, at their liturgies, they could sing once more of Yahweh's power (Psalm 48).

Scripture References

Abraham, the father of faith, placed total trust in the promises of Yahweh.
> Genesis 12:1-2
> 13:14-18
> 15:1-6
> 22:1-19

Trustfulness, faithfulness could be found again through turning from evil.
> Ezekiel 33:10-11
> Deuteronomy 4:28-31

Israel's faithfulness brought blessings; unfaithfulness brought trouble.
> Deuteronomy 11:18-32
> Psalms 52, 62

The ultimate result of faithfulness is the triumph of Yahweh's goodness.
> Isaiah 52:13-15
> Psalm 48

Discussion Questions

1. How did the Old Testament people understand faith?

2. How did Abraham demonstrate his faith?

3. What do I mean when I say "my faith"?

4. How can I daily nourish my life of faith?

5. What causes modern people to be faithless?

6. Why do we trust human resources so much more readily than we trust the Lord?

Prayer Service

All: In the name of the Father and of the Son and of the Holy Spirit. Amen.

Leader: Life comes to fulfillment to the extent that we place our trust in our loving Father. When we depend on less than him, we are insecure and unfulfilled. Let us reflect on the words of the prophet Isaiah.

Reader: *(Proclaims Isaiah 30:12-15.)*

Leader: Let us spend a few moments in silent meditation.

All: *(Pause to meditate.)*

Leader: Let us pray from Psalm 115.

All: Our trust is in you, O Lord.

Leader: Not by us, Yahweh, not by us, by you alone is glory deserved, by your love and your faithfulness! Do the pagans ask, "Where is their God?" Ours is the God whose will is sovereign in the heavens and on earth.

All: Our trust is in you, O Lord.

Leader: Whereas their idols, in silver and gold, products of human skill, have mouths, but never speak, eyes, but never see, ears, but never hear, noses, but never smell, hands, but never touch, feet, but never walk, and not a sound from their throats. Their makers will end up like them, and so will anyone who relies on them.

All: Our trust is in you, O Lord.

Leader: House of Israel, rely on Yahweh, on him, our help and shield! House of Aaron, rely on Yahweh, on him, our help and shield! You who fear Yahweh, rely on Yahweh, on him, our help and shield! Yahweh remembers us, he will bless, he will bless the House of Israel, he will bless the House of Aaron, he will bless those who fear Yahweh, without distinction of rank.

All: Our trust is in you, O Lord.

Leader: May Yahweh add to your numbers, yours and your children's too! May you be blessed by Yahweh, maker of heaven and earth! Heaven belongs to Yahweh, earth he bestows on man. The dead cannot praise Yahweh, they have gone down to silence; but we, the living, bless Yahweh henceforth and evermore.

All: Our trust is in you, O Lord.

Leader: Let us pray together:

All: Yahweh, our Father, we place our trust in you and your providential concern for us. May we never weaken and turn our faith to human ways but always seek your will and respond to your call. We pray in Jesus' name. Amen.

6
Faith in the New Testament

Background

In the Christian community, religious belief rested on the Old Testament awareness that salvation came through trusting God. In contrast to what many modern people think is Christian "faith" or "believing," the early community of Jesus lived faith as a religious experience. For them it was not merely holding on to a number of speculative truths. It was a continuous act of total confidence in Jesus as person, active in their life.

In the Gospel of John Jesus proclaims (6:37): "All that the Father gives me shall come to me; no one who comes to me will I ever reject." Faith is a person's free decision. But at the same time it is a gift from God to his people.

The New Testament often speaks of faith in "the name of the Lord." (See, for example, John 3:18.) Through Jesus' name, early Christians experienced his power and found eternal life (Mark 16:17-18). Yet their faith also had a specific content. The community members confess that Jesus has become the risen Lord through his Resurrection. Acceptance of this fact is the cornerstone of Christian belief (Romans 10:9-11). A fuller early formula of what the community believed is the creed in Philippians 2:6-11. To be among the people of the promise, the new Israel, one had to believe. Those who had faith in Jesus, no matter what nation they belonged to, were the true sons of Abraham (Romans 4:1-25; Galatians 3:5-9).

Christians also placed Baptism close to their notion of faith. Paul wrote to them in Ephesus (Ephesians 4:5): "There is one Lord, one faith, one baptism; one God and Father of all, who is over all, and works through all, and is in all." (Look also at Mark 16:16 and Acts 16:30-34.) Bringing people into salvation in the kingdom was accomplished through preaching, faith, and baptism (Matthew 28:19). A sample sermon is found in Acts 2:14-36. A person was baptized "in the name of the Lord" to show the union in Christ into which he or she was being introduced. Thereafter one's life was based on resurrection from sin to grace through the Spirit. Thus through Baptism, Jesus' name was both an object of preaching and a profession of faith (Acts 5:40, 8:12).

Faith in Jesus was not primarily confidence in him as a miracle worker. It was faith in his mission of saving the world and establishing the Father's kingdom. Miracles and exorcisms were signs that this was being done for the sinful. Jesus did not work miracles when faith was lacking. Indeed, he often said it was the person's faith that enabled the miracle to happen (Mark 5:34; Luke 7:50; Matthew 8:5-13, 13:58). Many of the Jews of Jesus' time were awed by his miracles but did not believe his message. Their lack of understanding and conversion brought judgment (John 12:44-48).

Mary was honored by the early community not only as the mother of Jesus but because of her faith. She was an early example of the true disciple. Her act of faith (Luke 1:45) was her righteousness. In the Gospel of Luke, her biological bond to Jesus is less important than her faith (Luke 8:19-21, 11:27-28). Faith was so central to discipleship that this basic quality in Mary symbolized the whole purpose of following Jesus.

In the Eucharist, the community celebrated the great mystery of faith. It manifested, above all, the presence of God in human actions (1 Corinthians 10:14-17). By participating in the Eucharist, they were in communion with the risen Lord and participants in his power to renew all of creation. Their faith in him was enlivened and renewed, and their fellowship with each other deepened.

Paul teaches that faith brings justification without anyone having to do anything to earn or deserve it (Romans 4:1-5; Ephesians 2:8-9). This refuted the Pharisee's doctrine that justification followed only if one perfectly fulfilled the law. Paul defines the worth of good works prior to God's free gift of justification. After its reception, however, faith is strengthened and brought alive by actions of love in Jesus' name (Galatians 3:25-29, 5:6).

Perseverance in faith was the basis of the spiritual life of the Christian community (1 Peter 5:8-9). A constant living out of Jesus' teachings was the Christian response to the gift of faith (John 8:31-32; 1 John 2:3-6).

When one was faith-full, one could do miracles as a sign of one's intimate union with Jesus in the kingdom (Matthew 17:19-20; Mark 16:17-18). Healing, both physical and spiritual, came through the faith of the community (James 5:13-16). Repentance resulted in renewed faith. The community plays a chief role in bringing the sinner back to a living faith (James 5:19-20).

Finally, 2 Thessalonians 2:15 reminds us that faith involves standing firmly in the traditions taught by the apostles.

Scripture References

Salvation comes through one Lord, one faith, one baptism.
> Mark 16:16
> Acts 16:30-34

Faith in the risen Lord is the cornerstone of Christian belief.
> Romans 10:9-11
> Philippians 2:6-11

Preaching, faith, and baptism are the means of extending the Lord's kingdom.
> Acts 2:14-36
> Matthew 28:19

Jesus' miracles called for interior conversion and faith.
> Mark 5:34
> Luke 7:50
> Matthew 8:5-13

In order to respond in faith, we must live the teachings of Jesus.
> John 8:31-32
> 1 John 2:3-6

Compare Paul and James' statements on faith and good works.
> Romans 4:1-5
> Ephesians 2:7-10
> James 2:4

Discussion Questions

1. Is faith in the risen Lord the basis of my Christianity?

2. What is so essential about faith? about preaching? about baptism?

3. Why did Jesus perform miracles?

4. What do we mean when we say that the Eucharist is the primary mystery of faith?

5. What experiences in my life have deepened my faith?

6. What teachings of Jesus do I find difficult to live?

7. How do my good works profess my faith in the Lord Jesus?

Prayer Service

All: In the name of the Father and of the Son and of the Holy Spirit. Amen.

Leader: We are joined to all ages of the followers of Jesus in placing our trust in his power and proclaiming him to be the Lord of our lives. Let us listen to why we place our trust in him.

Reader: *(Proclaims Philippians 2:6-11.)*

Leader: Let us meditate on these inspirational words of faith.

All: *(Meditate silently for a few moments.)*

Leader: Let us respond in faith with the words of Paul to the Colossians in chapter 3.

All: Our faith, O Lord, moves us to love!

Leader: You are God's chosen race, his saints; he loves you, and you should be clothed in sincere compassion, in kindness and humility, gentleness and patience.

All: Our faith, O Lord, moves us to love!

Leader: Bear with one another; forgive each other as soon as a quarrel begins. The Lord has forgiven you; now you must do the same.

All: Our faith, O Lord, moves us to love!

Leader: Over all these clothes, to keep them together and complete them, put on love. And may the peace of Christ reign in your hearts, because it is for this that you were called together as parts of one body. Always be thankful.

All: Our faith, O Lord, moves us to love!

Leader: Let the messsage of Christ, in all its richness, find a home with you. Teach each other, and advise each other, in all wisdom. With gratitude in your hearts sing psalms and hymns and inspired songs to God.

All: Our faith, O Lord, moves us to love!

Leader: And never say or do anything except in the name of the Lord Jesus, giving thanks to God the Father through him.

All: Our faith, O Lord, moves us to love!

Leader: Let us pray together:

All: Lord Jesus, you who placed total trust in your Father, have given us the way to live our faith in constant and loving service of each other. Give us your power to joyfully follow your way. Amen.

7
Worship in the Old Testament

Background

Three ideas — *work, service,* and *worship* — are expressed by the same Hebrew word, *'abad.* Work was worship of Yahweh. Worship was itself work for Yahweh, or service of Yahweh. Thus to worship meant far more than merely to "say prayers." It meant living the covenant to the fullest — giving praise to Yahweh and living with each other in kindness. The prophet Jeremiah reminded Israel: "In speaking to your fathers on the day I brought them out of the land of Egypt, I gave them no command concerning holocaust or sacrifice. This is rather what I commanded them: Listen to my voice; then I will be your God and you shall be my people. Walk in all the ways I command you, so that you may prosper" (Jeremiah 7:22-23).

Worship was the source of blessings. It reminded Israel of their humility and dependence on Yahweh. Yahweh would always respond to this frame of heart and mind by blessing his people. Psalm 88:17 is a typical expression of this understanding: "Grant me a proof of your favor, that my enemies may see, to their confusion, that you, O Lord, have helped and comforted me." The same stance is found in the beautiful priestly blessing found in Numbers 6:22-27. It begins: "The Lord said to Moses: 'Speak to Aaron and his sons and tell them: This is how you shall bless the Israelites . . .' " You will want to read the rest.

When we read a passage like Genesis 18:16-33, we can see that Israelite prayer was often a dialogue with Yahweh, a conversation which described Yahweh's feelings and thoughts, as well as the thoughts and needs of the Israelites. 1 Samuel 1:9-18 tells the moving story of Hannah at the shrine, praying for a son. Her prayer speaks of misery, pain, and utter dependence on Yahweh's love and mercy. It manifests great faith in his promises and acceptance of his will. After her son Samuel's birth, Hannah's prayer of thanksgiving becomes a kind of model for Mary's Magnificat (1 Samuel 2:1-10; Luke 1:46-55).

The early Hebrews built altars and offered sacrifices to God. Noah is an example (Genesis 8:20). The great ancestors of Israel, like Abraham (Genesis 12:7-8) and Jacob (Genesis 35:1-3), worshiped at altars. Moses established an important form of worship which entailed consulting the Lord about people's needs; Exodus 33:7 recalls how Moses used to pitch a "meeting tent." Anyone who wished to consult with the Lord would enter this tent. Moses himself often met "face-to-face" with the Lord in this meeting tent.

Worship and sacrifice usually followed a religious experience in which Israel saw the manifestation of Yahweh's power. Reminded of their unity with Yahweh, they would praise and thank him for his power and acknowledge their total dependence on him.

The great Exodus event was concluded with a worship celebration on Mount Sinai when the covenant was ratified by the Hebrews (Exodus 24:1-8). From this historical moment, the traditional basis for prayer was Israel's faith in Yahweh's promise that he would always be their God and protector. They were so sure of his care that their prayers of petition often concluded by praising him for having already answered the petition (Psalm 54).

Prayer was primarily a shared ritual due to Israel's sense of community. The Temple became the central place of public worship. Shrines were built throughout Israel as local houses of prayer. Though prayer could be offered anywhere, a custom grew that one should face the Temple in Jerusalem to pray (1 Kings 8:38), for there God dwelled in the midst of his people. 1 Kings chapter 6 describes the building of the Temple in Jerusalem in the days of King Solomon. For the Israelites it was the place of Yahweh's presence, as the meeting tent had been in the days of their wanderings (Exodus 40). Yahweh reminded his people, however, that his dynamic power was not found only in the Temple or the meeting tent, but in the midst of his community as they lived the covenant. 1 Kings 6:11, for example, makes this explicit.

The prayer-songs of Israel are the Psalms. Their themes are many and varied. They include the popular beliefs of Israel from the time of the kings to the return from exile in Babylon. They express in song-prayer the fundamental belief that Yahweh is a God of power and the Savior of Israel. They recall his saving them out of Egypt. Yahweh is merciful, forgiving, and faithful to his people and to individuals within the community. In the Psalms humankind is portrayed as weak, totally dependent on the mercy and will of Yahweh, in need of deliverance from sin. The Psalms were the liturgical prayers of Israel, sung in the Temple celebrations, as well as at local shrines.

Sacrifices were the central rite of Israel's worship. The sacrificial victim or offering was a gift to Yahweh. The gift was destroyed by fire so that it was irrevocably Yahweh's and could no longer be used by the people or the offerer. The community's sharing in the burnt offering by consuming it (or by having the priests do so) was a pledge of communion with Yahweh, just as our meals with one another can be the seal of our loyalty and friendship.

There were different types of sacrifice, which included:

The *burnt offering,* the oldest form, in which the victim was completely consumed by fire (Genesis 8:20).

The *peace sacrifice,* which was offered at all the great feasts. (The choicest parts of the burnt offering were saved for Yahweh. The rest was eaten before the altar, a sacred banquet — Deuteronomy 12:5-8).

The *sacrifice of obligation* was offered by the farming community. Cereal (the firstfruits of the harvest) was mixed with wine and incense and burned.

A *sacrifice of reparation* was offered for any offense or sin (Leviticus 5:14-26).

In the *memorial sacrifice* of "consumed dishes," food was placed apart for Yahweh as a memorial of the sacrifice and as a sign that the sacrifice was prolonged. The New Testament sacrifice of the Eucharist is reminiscent of this Hebrew tradition (Exodus 25:30).

Sacrifices of thanksgiving were also frequent (Psalms 107:22, 116:17).

The prophets supported the religious worship of the Temple, but only conditionally. They strongly protested against the community when it emphasized sacrificial rites and similar practices while violating social justice and love of neighbor. Amos cried out against such rites (Amos 5:21-26) because Israel has substituted them for justice. Isaiah 1:10-17 decried the sin of the people by calling them people of Sodom and protested against sacrifices offered in the midst of evil. You may look also at Hosea 5:6-7. This insistence on interior worship expressed in deeds flows throughout the Old Testament as consistently as do descriptions of the rites themselves. Even 1 Samuel 15:22-23 makes these connections.

So the Israelites were deeply worshipful. Their history had shown them that without Yahweh they could not exist. They had a deep, powerful desire to stay in union with their God, even though they struggled and were often confused in the attempt. Worship was a means of growth toward Yahweh, toward further experience of his love and power.

Scripture References

Israelite prayer was often a personal dialogue with Yahweh.

Genesis 18:16-33
Jeremiah 1:4-13

Worship reminded the community of Israel of Yahweh's faithfulness and the community's dependence on him.

Exodus 24:3-8
Psalm 116:1-9
Psalm 146

The Temple represented the place of Yahweh's presence, though he was always in their midst.
    1 Kings 6:11-13

The prophets warned that the only acceptable worship was spelled out in justice and charity.
    Isaiah 1:10-17
    Hosea 5:6-7
    1 Samuel 15:22-23

Discussion Questions

1. What religious experiences did Israel recall in worship?

2. What was the significance of the Psalms in Israelite worship?

3. Of what importance was the Temple in the worship in Israel?

4. Compare the symbolic meaning of Israel's sacrifices to our idea of sacrifice today.

5. Is my personal prayer a dialogue between me and the Lord? How can it become so?

6. What attitudes and feelings do I have when I pray or worship?

7. Why do many modern people find it difficult to pray? Do I share any of these difficulties? Why?

Prayer Service

All: In the name of the Father and of the Son and of the Holy Spirit. Amen.

Leader: When we pray we can rely on God's love and mercy. We need not bind God to our wishes, for he knows what is best for us better than we do. We need not bargain for his love because it is a free gift he gives to us when we come humbly before him in worship. Let us reflect on these ideas as we hear the attitude of prayer of Hannah, as told in the Old Testament.

Reader: *(Proclaims 1 Samuel 1:19-27, 2:1-11.)*

Leader: Let us pause to reflect on this prayerful faith of this great woman in our Jewish ancestry.

All: *(Meditate in silence for a few moments.)*

Leader: Let us respond by praying from Psalm 25.

All: The Lord is kindness and compassion.

Leader: I rely on you, do not let me be shamed, do not let my enemies gloat over me! No, those who hope in you are never shamed, shame awaits disappointed traitors.

All: The Lord is kindness and compassion.

Leader: Yahweh, make your ways known to me, teach me your paths. Set me in the way of your truth, and teach me, for you are the God who saves me. All day long I hope in you because of your goodness, Yahweh. Remember your kindness, Yahweh, your love, that you showed long ago.

All: The Lord is kindness and compassion.

Leader: Yahweh is so good, so upright, he teaches the way to sinners; in all that is right he guides the humble, and instructs the poor in his way.

All: The Lord is kindness and compassion.

Leader: Let us pray together:

All: Yahweh, our Father, listen as we turn to you in humble adoration and praise. We praise you for your constant faithfulness to us, your children. We pray for your guidance that we may always seek your will and respond in thanksgiving to your wonderful works. We pray in Jesus' name. Amen.

8
Worship in the New Testament

Background

Feast days were the special days of shared worship for our Jewish ancestors in the faith. The feasts were reenactments of Yahweh's saving deeds. By celebrating them, the Jews experienced anew the saving power of Yahweh. The Gospel of John teaches that we experience the saving power of Yahweh in our midst, in Jesus himself. We celebrate in and through the person of Jesus, the risen Lord and Messiah. John stresses that Jesus fulfilled the feasts of Judaism. The Gospel uses the presence of Jesus at each feast to explain the meaning of this fulfillment (John 2:13-22, 5:1-18, 7:2,37-38; 10:22-30; and chapter 13 and following). The ancient feasts looked forward to the total presence of God among his people. Through the Holy Spirit, Jesus was always in the presence of his community. The celebration of the liturgy of the Eucharist was and is the fulfillment of all the Jewish feasts of old.

The evangelists stressed the relationship between the Passover and the death and Resurrection of Jesus. The earlier festive celebration and memorial of the Israelites was a foreshadowing of the Passion of Jesus, who became our new Passover (Matthew 26:19,26-29; Mark 14; Luke 22; John 13-19).

The Christian community worships in "spirit and in truth," thus fulfilling the symbolic worship of our Jewish ancestors (John 4:21-24). Such inner worship is more important than any feast or place of prayer. So the Temple in Jerusalem was replaced by the Temple of Jesus himself. Each person baptized in Jesus' Spirit became the "temple of the Spirit of Jesus" (1 Corinthians 3:16-17). Therefore, prayers offered in each heart were offered in the presence of the Lord.

Christian liturgy then takes place in the presence of the Spirit. The worshiping community reenacts Jesus' Passion and Resurrection and is gathered completely into this saving action. The liturgy of the Eucharist is more than an act of adoration and remembrance. It is the prayer of thanksgiving for a work already accomplished — salvation through Jesus of all people everywhere. Hebrews chapter 9 compares the Old Testament sacrificial worship with that of Jesus. Jesus is the altar, the sacrifice which brings total union between Yahweh and his people (Hebrews 13:10-15). The Eucharist is celebrated "in remembrance of me" — of Jesus — which extends the reality of the mystery beyond time (1 Corinthians 11:23-26).

A sign of Jesus' Messiahship was his precedence over the Sabbath. He is the Lord of the Sabbath. Being more important than the day itself, he becomes the focal point of each act of Christian worship. Gradually the early community replaced worshiping on the Sabbath with Sunday worship, because it was the day of the Lord's Resurrection (Acts 20:7).

Jesus was the man of worship and prayer. His example of prayerfulness testified powerfully to the necessity of worship and prayer for his followers.

In prayer, Jesus called God his Father. He acknowledged his Father's supremacy, his Father's gift of new life to his people, and he recognized his own divine sonship. This is beautifully expressed in Jesus' own priestly prayer (John chapter 17).

Jesus often prayed in solitude, in the garden or on a mountain. For him, prayer was a deeply personal encounter with his Father (Mark 1:35; Matthew 14:23).

Jesus prayed for power and guidance at every important step of his life: his baptism, his choice of the twelve, his Passion, etc. (Luke 3:21, 6:12-13, 22:41). Jesus prayed in praise (Matthew 11:25-27). In prayer he sought his Father's will in the actions that he himself was living (Matthew 26:39-43).

As the ancient Israelites turned their eyes toward the Temple in Jerusalem to pray, Jesus lifted his eyes heavenward to the omnipresence of Yahweh (Mark 6:41).

Jesus' confidence that his Father heard his prayers can be seen clearly in the passage about the raising of Lazarus from the dead. John 11:39-43 tells the story.

Jesus taught his disciples that they too could pray completely assured of being heard, for his Father relates to us all as his children (Matthew 7:7-11). Jesus frequently reminded his community to pray persistently (Luke 18:1-8) and promised that their prayers would never go unheard (Luke 11:5-13). He stressed particularly that when two or three gathered in his name, he and his Father and the Spirit would be with them (Matthew 18:19-20). In fact, Jesus taught that his Father will grant whatever is asked for in Jesus' name because the Father loves those who love his Son (John 16:23,26-27).

The depth of mystical prayer is manifested in Jesus' prayer-experience at the Transfiguration (Luke 9:28-30).

Prayer in the New Testament, as in the Old, is a dialogue between God and his people. Our prayer relies on the power of the name of the Lord. Our petitions are granted through our humility before God and our acceptance of his will in our lives. Jesus himself gave us a pattern for prayer: the Our Father in Matthew 6:9-13 and Luke 11:2-4.

Christian worship and prayer is not merely an individual act, but the Spirit himself crying out the prayer of Jesus — "Abba, Father" — in each Christian heart and in the faithful community (Romans 8:14-16; Galatians 4:6).

The Old Testament cultic sacrifice for sin has been accomplished, once for all, by Jesus in his Passion and Resurrection. Now the Spirit is in our midst empowering the forgiveness of sin, without which true worship would be impossible (John 20:19-23).

To be effective, our prayer must extend the Lord's care through our actions. The Lord empowers us, in unity with him, to be his instruments of love, compassion, and aid to one another. James says, "If a man who does not control his tongue imagines that he is devout, he is self-deceived; his worship is pointless. Looking after orphans and widows in their distress and keeping oneself unspotted by the world make for pure worship without stain before our God and Father" (James 1:26).

Prayer and worship are the channel for the Lord's power in our daily existence. Through prayer the Christian community is strengthened by the Spirit, grows into a deeper knowledge of the Lord, is motivated to do good works, and is given the ability to face any situation in security and joy (Colossians 1:9-14).

The New Testament teaches that when we pray, we can count on Saint Paul's insight: "For I am certain that neither death nor life, neither angels nor principalities, neither the present nor the future, nor powers, neither height nor depth nor any other creature, will be able to separate us from the love of God that comes to us in Christ Jesus, our Lord" (Romans 8:38-39).

Scripture References

Jesus' Passion and Resurrection fulfill the ancient Passover.
1 Corinthians 5:7-8

Read the comparison of Israelite sacrificial worship and Jesus' mission.
Hebrews 9:1-28, 13:9-15

The Eucharist extends the mystery of Jesus beyond time.
1 Corinthians 11:23-26

Jesus was a man of prayer.
John 17
Luke 3:21, 6:12-13, 22:41
Matthew 11:25-27

Jesus teaches us to trust our prayers will be heard.
> Matthew 7:7-11, 18:19-20
> Luke 11:5-13
> John 16:23, 26-27

Prayer is our source of strength in times of difficulty.
> Colossians 1:9-14

Discussion Questions

1. How is Jesus the fulfillment of all the ancient Israelite feasts?

2. What do we mean when we say that Jesus is the new Temple?

3. How is Jesus the perfect sacrifice fulfilling the sacrificial offerings of Israel?

4. Why is the liturgy of the Eucharist the primary worship of the Christian community?

5. Why did Jesus pray? Do I pray for the same reason?

6. According to Jesus, why can we be assured that all of our prayers will be heard?

7. How is my prayer extended into my daily actions?

8. Why do we not trust that our prayers will be heard?

9. How does worship and prayer help me to cope with problems and difficulties?

Prayer Service

All: In the name of the Father and of the Son and of the Holy Spirit. Amen.

Leader: We believe that the Lord hears our prayers. We believe that through prayer we are given the power of Jesus to overcome all evil and to find solutions for all problems. Let us listen with confidence to Paul's words which remind us of this.

Reader: *(Proclaims Colossians 1:9-14.)*

Leader: Let us meditate silently for a few moments on this promise.

All: *(Meditate silently for a few moments.)*

Leader: Let us respond to this revelation by praying from Psalm 138.

All: We give you thanks, O Lord, for you listen to our needs.

Leader: I thank you, Yahweh, with all my heart, because you have heard what I said. In the presence of the angels I play for you, and bow down toward your holy Temple.

All: We give you thanks, O Lord, for you listen to our needs.

Leader: I give thanks to your name for your love and faithfulness; your promise is even greater than your fame. The day I called for help, you heard me and you increased my strength.

All: We give you thanks, O Lord, for you listen to our needs.

Leader: Though I live surrounded by trouble, you keep me alive — to my enemies' fury! You stretch your hand out and save me, your right hand will do everything for me. Yahweh, your love is everlasting, do not abandon us whom you have made.

All: We give you thanks, O Lord, for you listen to our needs.

Leader: Let us pray together:

All: Lord Jesus, you are our strength in time of affliction. You are the source of our power and our joy and fulfillment. May we always turn to you in prayer with confidence and thanksgiving, praising your overwhelming love and kindness. May we extend your compassion and love to all you send along our way. May we come to be with you in eternity where all praise and honor is yours forever and ever. Amen.

9
Holiness in the Old Testament

Background

The root of the word *holiness* means "to set apart." Israel practiced a "holy" religion since Yahweh revealed himself as other than, separate from, his creation.

In contrast to pagan gods, Yahweh was not a mere personification of the national spirit, who could be forgotten or changed by the people's whims. He also could not be controlled by magic; he was not dependent on his people. He was holy in himself.

Israel was also "set apart" from all other people to manifest Yahweh's power and will to all nations. Israel was to know and express Yahweh, the One, the Holy, and to worship him alone.

The root meaning of holiness is otherness, separateness from the common and profane. But the holiness of Israel also affirms that the people belonged to and were consecrated to God. So the holy nation of Israel was "separate" from the pagan world in the sense that Israel was uniquely consecrated to and possessed by Yahweh. Thus Israel was capable of worshiping a holy God.

Yahweh affirmed that he was God, not man, and uniquely holy by nature (Hosea 11:9). He was radically different from idols. His holiness was alive and powerful, so that humans could not come too close without being consumed (Exodus 3:1-6). His holiness is manifested in his creation, judgment, and salvation (Isaiah 40:25-26; Ezekiel 36:23-28). The places where Yahweh appeared became holy because of his presence: the burning bush, the appearance of the divine messenger to Joshua near Jericho (Joshua 5:13-15), the land of Canaan (Psalm 78:51-55), the city of Jerusalem (Psalm 46:5), the Temple (Psalm 5:8). In short, every place where direct contact with Yahweh was experienced was seen as continuously participating in his holiness.

Yahweh's holiness is revealed by what he does. Not only does he save his people to set them apart as his chosen ones, but he sanctifies them despite their sins. Sin made them profane and common; his power brought them holiness (Numbers 20:12-13). In the history of his people, when Yahweh restores Israel from calamity, he manifests his holiness by reestablishing order, by making his will supreme and overpowering evil (Isaiah 29:18-23). The people's redemption from tragedy was a witness to the nations of Yahweh's holiness (Ezekiel 20:41). As long as Israel was obedient, Yahweh protected it from outside assault because Israel belonged to him and was therefore holy. Jeremiah 2:3 proclaims: "Sacred to the Lord was Israel, the first fruits of his harvest; should anyone presume to partake of them, evil would befall him."

Yahweh demanded that his people be holy because he was holy (Leviticus 11:43-45). Holiness comes to creatures simply because of their union with the divine. Israel was to proclaim the holiness, the "otherness," of Yahweh and to make clear that Yahweh is not of the same nature as his creatures, even though he is close to them.

The name *Yahweh* was the holiest of the names of Israel's God. When his people acted in a manner unworthy of his name, failed to confess his holiness, or prevented others from doing so, they "profaned the holy name." In Leviticus we see that an early protest against child sacrifice and the prohibition of all similar extremities was based on Yahweh's holy name (Leviticus 20:1-8, 22:1).

Isaiah 6:1-10 expresses graphically the power of Yahweh to purge sin from the prophet (and likewise from all Israel) and to raise the prophet to holiness in unity with himself. This passage also suggests how, for Isaiah, holiness implies his vocation: to become Yahweh's messenger to the nation.

Liturgical worship reminded Israel that they were a holy people who were able to communicate with and participate in the holiness and power of Yahweh. Israel belonged to Yahweh initially simply by his choice of them, expressed forever in his covenant with them (Exodus 19:5-6).

To share in the liturgical rites one had to prepare himself by purification. This symbolized that he was leaving the profane and entering a deep relationship with the divine. The purification or "cleansing" rite was done in different ways. It often included the offering of a special sacrifice or washing with water (Numbers 19:7-10, for example). All of the material things used in the cultic worship represented Yahweh's presence and power. From this association with worship, these persons and things became part of Yahweh's holiness, and were therefore "set apart for holy use." Included were the priests, the offerings and sacrificial victims, the altar, vestments, furniture, vessels. Exodus chapter 29 describes a ritual and mentions many of the holy objects.

In the Old Testament, holiness is not the same concept as morality. Though morality flowed from holiness, they were two distinct things. The Israelites were holy because God possessed them. The holiness of Israel was a gift from Yahweh. The expression of that holiness meant that the Israelite community was supposed to live morally. Morality proclaimed the holy nature of their God and the holiness he had bestowed upon Israel. Chapter 19 of Leviticus sets up a moral plan by which Israel could preserve and demonstrate its election to holiness. Note especially the opening two verses. All the demands of goodness and for ritual are based on the holiness of Yahweh. Holy was what he was in himself and, therefore, what his people were.

Scripture References

Yahweh is holy.
> Hosea 11:9
> Exodus 3:1-6

Yahweh's holiness is seen in his creative, salvific actions toward Israel.
> Isaiah 40:25-26
> Ezekiel 36:23-28

Israel's vocation was to proclaim the holiness of Yahweh.
> Numbers 20:12-13
> Leviticus 11:43-45
> Ezekiel 20:41

When Israel sinned they profaned the holiness of Yahweh. Yahweh would cleanse them so that his holiness could be seen.
> Leviticus 20:1-8, 22:1
> Isaiah 6:1-5

Cultic worship involved rites of purification to preserve its holy nature.
> Exodus 29

Moral living was the practical way Israel expressed its holiness, beloved by Yahweh.
> Leviticus 19

Discussion Questions

1. What are the basic meanings of holiness in the Old Testament?

2. Why was it important in a pagan environment that Yahweh's "separateness" be proclaimed?

3. Why did Yahweh choose Israel to be a "holy people, a priestly nation"?

4. How are holiness and morality different yet connected in Old Testament thought?

5. How can I proclaim God's holiness to the modern world?

6. What does it mean to me personally that God has called me to holiness?

7. How does my way of living express my belief in God? If people see me, what kind of God do they think I believe in?

Prayer Service

All: In the name of the Father and of the Son and of the Holy Spirit. Amen.

Leader: Yahweh chooses us to be a holy people to proclaim to the world his holiness. When we follow his commandments and depend on his power, we live in unity with him and bring holiness to creation. Let us reflect on the message of the prophet Ezekiel.

Reader: *(Proclaims Ezekiel 36:23-28.)*

Leader: Let us meditate on these sacred words.

All: *(Meditate in silence for a few moments.)*

Leader: Let us respond to this revelation by praying Psalm 99.

All: We praise your awesome and holy name, O Lord.

Leader: Yahweh is king, the nations tremble; he is enthroned on the cherubs, earth quakes; Yahweh is great in Zion. He is high over all nations; may they praise your great and terrible name, "Holy is he, and mighty!"

All: We praise your awesome and holy name, O Lord.

Leader: You are a king who loves justice, insisting on honesty, justice, virtue, as you have done for Jacob. Let us extol Yahweh our God, and worship at his footstool, "Holy is he!"

All: We praise your awesome and holy name, O Lord.

Leader: Moses, Aaron one of his priests, and Samuel his votary, all invoked Yahweh: and he answered them. He talked with them in the pillar of cloud; they obeyed his decrees, the Law he gave them.

All: We praise your awesome and holy name, O Lord.

Leader: Yahweh our God, you responded to them, a God of forgiveness for them, in spite of punishing their sins. Extol Yahweh our God, worship at his holy mountain, "Holy is Yahweh our God!"

All: We praise your awesome and holy name, O Lord.

Leader: Let us pray together:

All: We praise you, Lord our God, for calling us into your holiness and for forgiving us our sins that we might manifest to others the power of your love. May we always remain in your lordship and your holiness and be your messengers to all nations. We pray in Jesus' name. Amen.

10
Holiness in the New Testament

Background

The New Testament speaks of holiness in the same way the Old Testament did. God is the holy Father (John 17:11), his law and covenant are holy (Romans 7:12). His temple, the people of God, and the new Jerusalem are holy (1 Corinthians 3:17; Revelation 21:2). 1 Timothy 4:4-5 teaches that all creation is holy when it is seen as a reflection of God's holiness: "Everything God created is good; nothing is to be rejected when it is received with thanksgiving, for it is made holy by God's word and by prayer."

The New Testament sees Israel's vocation to holiness completed in Jesus, the Holy One of God. Jesus' holiness is in his divine sonship and the presence of the Spirit of God in him; he is conceived by the Holy Spirit and will be called the Holy One, the Son of God (Luke 1:35). At his baptism, Jesus is anointed by the Holy Spirit (Luke 3:22; Acts 10:38). Jesus is called the "holy servant of God" (Acts 4:27,30) who by his Passion, death, and Resurrection is uniquely consecrated and holy to God. Therefore his Father exalted him (Philippians 2:9).

Jesus' holiness was not the fruit of human goodness or acts of virtue, but rather his participation in the holiness and divinity of his Father (John 14:10-11). Jesus' holiness is manifested when he drives out unclean spirits from people and the spirits call him "the Holy One of God" (Mark 1:23-27 and Luke 4:33-35). Jesus and his apostles were sanctified so that their demonstration of the power of the Father would be fruitful (John 17:17-19). Thus, Jesus imparted to his beloved friends his own fullness of holiness so that he would remain for all time in complete union with them.

In the Old Testament, moral goodness flowed from holiness. In the same way, Jesus' goodness sprang from his holiness. He loved; he urged others to love. He did many healing works. He forgave sin, a continuous act to overcome the powerful effects of sin in creation. All these pointed toward the re-creation of people into their original unity with their Creator-Father.

Pentecost — the infilling of the Christian community by the Holy Spirit — is the key event which empowers Christians with the holiness of the risen Lord. It flowered into the vocation of Jesus' followers to go forth and proclaim his holiness to all nations.

The holiness of the Christian community means that we are separate — set apart from the world of sin, dedicated to God — by faith in the risen Lord. We are God's chosen ones (Colossians 3:12). We inherit the riches of his glory (Ephesians 1:18), demonstrated in our vision and power.

Romans 6:3-4 explains how, through Baptism and faith, we are received into a new life which is the community of the Lord. In this new life we experience forgiveness of sins, which frees us to be holy as we share in his holiness (1 Corinthians 6:11; 1 Peter 2:9; Ephesians 1:3-5). This is but the beginning of a growing manifestation of God's will in our lives. We may continuously express holiness by seeking out and following God's will (Romans 12:1-2). 1 Corinthians 1:30 sums up the new life in Christ: he *is* our holiness — which is why the early community of Jesus was referred to as "saints." They had been sanctified by Jesus in them. In this holy life, hope and confidence are constant virtues of Christians. They express the absolute assurance of the power of the holiness of Jesus and our intimate union with that power.

Early Christians practiced the custom of greeting each other with a "holy embrace." It recalled their union in holiness with each other and with the Lord. A common greeting was, "May the grace of our Lord Jesus Christ be with you" (1 Thessalonians 5:26-28).

As for Jesus, so for his community: holiness is the basis for morality. But they are not the same. God continues to demonstrate his holiness in his works of mercy as well as through the moral living of his people (1 Thessalonians 4:1-12). The Christian community — and thus each of its baptized members — is holy simply because of its unity with Jesus, who is holy. Living morally demonstrates this holy nature to others. Simultaneously, morality sustains holiness within each Christian (1 Peter 1:13-16). Each Christian is a holy temple because the Holy Spirit dwells within him (1 Corinthians 3:16-17).

In the New Testament, the cultic aspects of holiness all but disappear. The emphasis is on the personal, moral aspects of holiness. Cultic worship — liturgy and sacraments — symbolize holiness on a more spiritual level. The purification of external things in Old Testament practice becomes the purification of human hearts, necessary since we are the temple of the Lord with Jesus, the sacrificial offering to the Father (2 Corinthians 7:1). United in the Lord in the Eucharistic liturgy, Christians can offer God true worship by offering themselves through Jesus' holy offering. This both fulfills and makes unnecessary the ancient cultic worship of the Israelites (Romans 12:1).

Scripture References

Israel's vocation to be holy is completed in Jesus.
> Hebrews 9:1-14

The holiness of Jesus.
> Luke 1:35, 3:22, 4:33-35
> Mark 1:22
> Acts 4:27, 30
> John 14:10-11

The Christian community is holy because it is in Jesus. It is separate from sin, is the chosen race, and inheritor of his richness.
> Acts 26:18
> Colossians 3:12
> Ephesians 1:19

Moral living manifests holiness.
> 1 Peter 1:13-16
> 1 Thessalonians 4:1-12

United in holiness with Jesus, the community can offer true cultic worship.
> Romans 12:1

Discussion Questions

1. How is Israel's call to holiness completed in Jesus?

2. How did Jesus demonstrate holiness? Can I do the same? How?

3. Why is Pentecost the key event for the Christian community?

4. What do we mean that the Christian community is holy?

5. What is the connection between holiness and morality in the New Testament?

6. What is the difference between Old Testament cultic worship and cultic worship in the New Testament?

7. Does my personal union with Jesus make me holy? How does it show?

8. What actions of the Christian community prevent the world from knowing the holiness of God?

9. Why do so many people shy away from appearing to be "holy Joes"?

Prayer Service

All: In the name of the Father and of the Son and of the Holy Spirit. Amen.

Leader: God has called us to growth in holiness. We grow daily in holiness by our actions that unite us with the loving and holy way of the Lord's life. Let us listen to the words Paul addresses to the Thessalonians.

Reader: *(Proclaims 1 Thessalonians 4:1-12.)*

Leader: Let us meditate on these words.

All: *(Meditate in silence for a few moments.)*

Leader: Let us respond to the Scriptures by praying Psalm 112.

All: The blessings of the Lord's holiness are upon us.

Leader: Happy the man who fears Yahweh by joyfully keeping his commandments! Children of such a man will be powers on earth, descendants of the upright will always be blessed.

All: The blessings of the Lord's holiness are upon us.

Leader: There will be riches and wealth for his family, and his righteousness can never change. For the upright he shines like a lamp in the dark, he is merciful, tenderhearted, virtuous.

All: The blessings of the Lord's holiness are upon us.

Leader: Interest is not charged by this good man, he is honest in all his dealings. Kept safe by virtue, he is ever steadfast, and leaves an imperishable memory behind him.

All: The blessings of the Lord's holiness are upon us.

Leader: With constant heart, and confidence in Yahweh, he need never fear bad news. Steadfast in heart he overcomes his fears: in the end he will triumph over his enemies.

All: The blessings of the Lord's holiness are upon us.

Leader: Quick to be generous, he gives to the poor, his righteousness can never change, men such as this will always be honored, though this fills the wicked with fury until, grinding their teeth, they waste away, vanishing like their vain hopes.

All: The blessings of the Lord's holiness are upon us.

Leader: Let us pray together:

All: Lord Jesus, you not only create holiness in us but empower us with your Spirit to live holy lives. May we always rest in your holiness and strive to manifest it every day in every way. We give you thanks forever and ever. Amen.

11
Justice in the Old Testament

Background

In Hebrew society, justice extended beyond simple equality or retribution. It meant benevolent generosity among the chosen people, especially toward the underprivileged. So states Proverbs 31:9: "Open your mouth, decree what is just, defend the needy and the poor!" Justice is closely related to mercy — *hesed* in Hebrew. The word also includes notions of compassion, patience, and forgiveness.

Yahweh is the "God of *hesed*" who always assisted his people, because he had formed the Sinai covenant with Israel. Likewise among the Israelites, *hesed* was the primary expression of that covenant. The people of Yahweh assisted one another in *hesed*.

The prophets of Israel came to understand that it took deep faith and trust to live justly. They saw that Yahweh's justice toward them was their pattern for justice. So the prophets exhorted the people to seek his way first — then justice would be possible in this world (Amos 5:23-24; Isaiah 51:1-8). So the Israelite did not act justly from human sentiments alone. The Spirit of Yahweh in his servants produced justice and mercy in society. Acts of love and mercy were synonymous with acts of justice (Hosea 2:21).

Yahweh's justice toward his covenant people did not depend on their observance of covenant obligations. Yahweh treated his people justly because he was just in himself. They called him the Just One — he would not violate himself or his own word, regardless of how his people behaved. Nehemiah recalls this, saying in prayer: "In all that has come upon us, you have been just, for you kept faith while we have done evil" (9:32-34).

From early times, Israel knew that Yahweh's justice was his loving care for the salvation of his people, in their practical everyday lives as well as spiritually. His great works on their behalf manifested his justice (Judges 5:8-11). Knowing his care for them, Israel expected Yahweh to bring about the kingdom where "kindness and truth shall meet; justice and peace shall kiss. Truth shall spring out of the earth, and justice shall look down from heaven" (Psalm 85:11-12).

Nevertheless, Yahweh condemned Israel for refusing to heed his designs, for not keeping their part of the covenant. In reviewing the catastrophes that had come to Israel as a result, Zechariah 7:9-12 uses strong language. Yet the prophets are full of witness to the evil that remained among them. Micah 2:1-3 is an example.

Yet, when punishment came in the form of affliction, Yahweh's justice was ready to restore Israel's society. When Israel was repentant, Yahweh was forgiving. He aided the afflicted ones (even if they had brought their troubles on themselves) because he was the Creator. As he had given them life, so he desired to remove stumbling blocks from their lives (Isaiah 57:14-19).

As Yahweh was just, he reminded the Israelites that they must not be unjust to each other, regardless of any injustice they might have received. Micah puts it precisely: "You have been told, O man, what is good, and what the Lord requires of you: Only to do the right and to love goodness, and to walk humbly with your God" (Micah 6:8).

David was a good example of Israelite justice — at least sometimes. Yahweh's pattern was alive in him. When Saul was still king, he had become an enemy of David. He kept trying to capture and kill David. When David found himself in a situation where he could easily kill Saul, he refused because Saul was the "anointed one." Even Saul admitted that David was more just than he, for David had shown Saul kindness in exchange for Saul's evil intent against him (1 Samuel 24).

Later, the prophets struggled to keep Yahweh's pattern of justice before the people. Isaiah 32:1-8 describes a just society. The good and not the tricksters would be honored and successful. Yahweh assured Israel that their worship was abominable to him unless it was matched with justice (Amos 5:23-25; Hosea 6:6; Psalm 50:5-23). The Israelites also fasted as a religious exercise to seek

Yahweh. Isaiah prophesied against their inconsistency in fasting while they did not seek justice (Isaiah 58:1-11; Zechariah 7:5-10).

A strong protest against injustice can be found in Isaiah 10:1-4. Ezekiel cried out that the only way to life was through justice (Ezekiel 18:5-9). Daniel was a later proponent of justice. He reminded King Nebuchadnezzar that he could atone for his sins by acting kindly toward the poor (Daniel 4:24).

The renowned teachers of Israel shared the prophets' concern for justice. In Sirach 4:1-10, they wrote that just actions make a person a "son of the Most High," loved by Yahweh with a "tender love." In Wisdom, chapters 2 and 3, we find a discussion of the relation of justice to suffering and death. (Here, too, we find some of the first intimations of a life after death — something which Hebrews did not always accept.) Chapters 4 and 5 continue the discussion, pointing out the judgments against wickedness to be expected in the afterlife. (See also Psalm 37.)

The expected Messiah was viewed as the ultimate bringer of justice (Isaiah 11:1-9, 42:1-8). The Messiah would rule justly, as a spiritual and actual descendant of David (Jeremiah 23:5), and the messianic kingdom would abound in justice (Jeremiah 23:6). Yahweh's people would be reestablished in a new kingdom, but this one would be just and therefore prosperous (Isaiah 56:1-8).

Thus Israel looked to Yahweh's covenant and his active power in their midst. He formed the basis and source of their growth in understanding and practice of justice. His pattern was compassion, hospitality, assistance to each other, and peace. Together, these were justice. When they lived justly, they prospered; when they lived unjustly, they floundered and were beset with military defeat and other tragedy. But through it all, Yahweh remained merciful, ever ready to restore them to himself.

Scripture References

To be just, the Israelite had to have faith and trust in Yahweh.
>Wisdom 1:1-2
>Isaiah 51:1-8

Yahweh was just because he aided the afflicted.
>Isaiah 57:14-19

Prayer and worship were worthless unless accompanied by justice.
>Amos 5:23-25

Prophecy pointed to the Messiah, who would reign with justice.
>Isaiah 11:1-8, 42:1-9
>Jeremiah 23:5-6

Discussion Questions

1. What is the Old Testament understanding of *hesed?*

2. How did Israel connect faith in Yahweh with the practice of justice?

3. How did Yahweh manifest his justice in Israel's experience?

4. Why was Israel called to be just to all the afflicted?

5. What causes modern people to be unjust?

6. How much do I trust God and how does this trust connect with my actions?

7. Why are the powerful and unjust so often honored in modern society?

Prayer Service

All: In the name of the Father and of the Son and of the Holy Spirit. Amen.

Leader: The Lord empowers us to extend his justice to all the world, so that he will be known and loved and salvation can come to every person. Let us listen to the words of the prophet Isaiah.

Reader: *(Proclaims Isaiah 51:1-8.)*

Leader: Let us pause to reflect on this message of the prophet.

All: *(Meditate in silence for a few moments.)*

Leader: Let us pray with words from Psalm 72 that speaks of the just kingdom of the Messiah.

All: May the justice of the Lord cover the world!

Leader: God, give your own justice to the king, your own righteousness to the royal son, so that he may rule your people rightly and your poor with justice. Let the mountains and hills bring a message of peace for the people. Uprightly he will defend the poorest, he will save the children of those in need, and crush their oppressors.

All: May the justice of the Lord cover the world!

Leader: Like sun and moon he will endure, age after age, welcome as rain that falls on the pasture, and showers to thirsty soil. In his days virtue will flourish, a universal peace till the moon is no more.

All: May the justice of the Lord cover the world!

Leader: His empire shall stretch from sea to sea, from the river to the ends of the earth. The Beast will cower before him and his enemies grovel in the dust; the kings of Tarshish and of the islands will pay him tribute. The kings of Sheba and Seba will offer gifts; all kings will do him homage, all nations become his servants.

All: May the justice of the Lord cover the world!

Leader: He will free the poor man who calls to him, and those who need help, he will have pity on the poor and feeble, and save the lives of those in need; he will redeem their lives from exploitation and outrage, their lives will be precious in his sight.

All: May the justice of the Lord cover the world!

Leader: Let us pray together:

All: God, our Father, may we be the instruments of your peace, compassion, and justice. We desire to spread your justice across our world and our time. May your kingdom come and may your love and justice be felt within the hearts of all people everywhere, so that glory and honor may be given to you, our Creator and Father. We pray in the name of Jesus, your Son. Amen.

12
Justice in the New Testament

Background

Jesus is the model of justice for his followers. The Letter to the Hebrews quotes Psalm 45:8 and sees it fulfilled in the person of Jesus: "You (Jesus) have loved justice and hated wickedness, therefore God, your God, has anointed you with the oil of gladness above your fellow kings" (Hebrews 1:9).

At the time of Jesus, the Pharisees had turned justice into a matter of rigidly keeping all the ritual laws of Judaism. Jesus taught against this interpretation. He declared that true justice was not an external ritual but a matter of the heart. If the heart was just, what flowed from it in action would also be just. Matthew 5:7 indicates that Jesus also accepted the Old Testament insistence on mercy. So Luke 6:27-38 extends Jesus' call for justice to the merciful service even of one's enemies. "Love your enemies, do good to those who hate you" . . . "When someone takes your coat, let him have your shirt as well" . . . "Give to all who beg from you" . . . "Do to others what you would have them do to you" . . . "Be compassionate, as your Father is compassionate." Clearly justice does not mean "giving him what he deserves." It means acting from love and mercy *regardless*. It means acting like Jesus.

Jesus forgave sins. Forgiveness *is* his justice. Forgiveness enables the sinner himself to practice justice in mercy and love. If one feels sinful, defensiveness prevents merciful action. But when one experiences forgiveness, one is free — and can be actively merciful. Luke 7:36-50 illustrates forgiveness at work in the freedom to love.

Jesus' parable of the lost sheep pointed out his overwhelming readiness to go out to each individual and bring all to the security and full-lifeness of his own flock, those whom he shepherds in love (Luke 15:1-7).

The parable of the wayward son exemplifies the limitlessness of the Father's mercy and justice. Joyful celebration is extended to the son who seeks the justice of his father. Not only is the son's sinfulness forgiven, but his needs (clothing, food, friends) are met in mercy and compassion (Luke 15:11-31).

Jesus did not mince words in his condemnation of the unjust. Luke 11:39-46 shouts out Jesus' words of judgment.

Jesus taught that his Father's final judgment will be based on whether or not we have practiced justice toward Jesus himself. If we have been merciful and compassionate to those who neither deserved nor expected it, we will belong forever to Jesus Christ. (Read Matthew 25:31-46.)

The foundation for justice in the Christian is expressed in Galatians 2:20: "And the life I live now is not my own; Christ is living in me. I still live my human life, but it is a life of faith in the Son of God, who LOVED ME AND GAVE HIMSELF FOR ME. I will not treat God's gracious gift as pointless." If Christ lives in the Christian, how can the Christian *not* live in mercy, both receiving and giving the justice of Jesus?

The Letter to the Philippians teaches that justice is the essence and goal of Christian life, and that it is Christ's work in us (Philippians 1:9-11).

The vocation of Christians "is not a matter of eating or drinking" — a reference to the ritual prescriptions of the Jews — "but of justice, peace, and the joy that is given by the Holy Spirit. Whoever serves Christ in this way pleases God and wins the esteem of men. Let us, then, make it our aim to work for peace and to strengthen one another" (Romans 14:17-19).

Christians are not to condemn those who transgress against them, for Jesus is forgiving of all transgressions. Christians are called to be ambassadors of Christ in the reconciliation of all people with their heavenly Father (2 Corinthians 5:18-19). Therefore, forgiveness is their necessity.

The Letter of James condemns discrimination among the saints of the early community. He points out the human tendency to prefer the well-favored to those less fortunate — and condemns it as merciless, that is, unjust. Treat all alike in love, he insists. "Merciless is the judgment on the man who has not shown mercy; but mercy triumphs over judgment" (James 2:1-13).

James also denounces faith in Christ and his power unless this faith is put into practice by just works. "If a brother or a sister has nothing to wear and no food for the day, and you say to them, 'Good-bye and good luck! Keep warm and well fed,' but do not meet their bodily needs, what good is that?" (James 2:14-17)

The Book of Revelation also announces how the good works by the Christian community are eternal, belonging to the life-style of the final kingdom of the Lord (Revelation 14:13).

Thus, the early Christians found in Jesus not only their model and inspiration but the power and strength to be just, to live lives of justice and mercy toward all. Life for the community meant proclaiming the wondrous mercy and salvation shown by the risen Lord. They praised him for enabling them to share in the justice of his kingdom. They demonstrated this ability by sharing their justice actively with others.

Scripture References

For Jesus, mercy is vital to life.
> Matthew 5:7

Jesus forgave sins so the practice of justice was possible for sinners.
> Luke 7:36-50

To be just to one another is to be just to Jesus himself.
> Matthew 25:31-46

Christians are called to be ambassadors of the justice of the Lord.
> 2 Corinthians 5:18-20

Living just lives brings us fulfillment here and in the hereafter.
> Revelations 14:13

Discussion Questions

1. How is justice connected with Jesus' forgiving of sins?

2. Why did Jesus extend justice to enemies?

3. What is the foundation on which Christians base justice? What people deserve? What Jesus did? Or . . .?

4. What is the teaching about justice in James?

5. Why do we not act justly to enemies? Why should we?

6. What injustices does the Lord condemn in our modern society? What is our stand in regard to these injustices?

7. Do I believe that my life really isn't mine but belongs to the Lord? Why or why not? Does my belief show in my decisions? How?

Prayer Service

All: In the name of the Father and of the Son and of the Holy Spirit. Amen.

Leader: The Lord teaches us that the only way we can be truly happy is if we follow his way. He spells out the basics of his living way in the Sermon on the Mount. Let us listen to these Beatitudes he teaches.

Reader: *(Proclaims Matthew 5:1-12.)*

Leader: Let us pause to reflect on the meaning of these Beatitudes in our own personal lives.

All: *(Pause for a few moments of reflection.)*

Leader: Let us pray with words from Psalm 92, praising the Lord for his justice toward us.

All: Your great works and teachings, O Lord, show forth your justice.

Leader: It is good to give thanks to Yahweh, to play in honor of your name, Most High, to proclaim your love at daybreak and your faithfulness all through the night to the music of the zither and lyre, to the rippling of the harp. I am happy, Yahweh, at what you have done; at your achievements I joyfully exclaim.

All: Your great works and teachings, O Lord, show forth your justice.

Leader: "Great are your achievements, Yahweh, immensely deep your thoughts!" Stupid men are not aware of this, fools can never appreciate it. The wicked may sprout as thick as weeds and every evil-doer flourish, but only to be everlastingly destroyed, whereas you are supreme for ever.

All: Your great works and teachings, O Lord, show forth your justice.

Leader: So the virtuous flourish like palm trees and grow as tall as the cedars of Lebanon. Planted in the house of Yahweh, they will flourish in the courts of our God, still bearing fruit in old age, still remaining fresh and green, to proclaim that Yahweh is righteous, my rock in whom no fault is to be found!

All: Your great works and teachings, O Lord, show forth your justice.

Leader: Let us pray together:

All: Lord Jesus, you have forgiven us and shown forth your mercy and justice to us. You have called us blessed when we live as you live and have filled us with deep peace and security. May we be able with your power to share your way with others and help to continue in the establishing of your kingdom on earth. We praise you in the Father and the Spirit forever. Amen.

13
Suffering in the Old Testament

Background

The problem of evil, suffering, and death is a key theme of every major philosophy and religion in the history of the world. Biblical religion tries to understand evil in the light of our experience of God's goodness. It tries to help believers to cope with pain and to find meaning and hope in the midst of suffering.

The basic teaching in the Old Testament about suffering is that its purpose is to bring people to examine their lives in terms of their relationship with Yahweh. Suffering reminds them how self-sufficiently they have been acting and how far they have drifted from their dependence on Yahweh. Suffering shows them that happiness can be found only in dependence on Yahweh and his saving power.

Our Hebrew ancestors believed that God created the world good, not evil (Genesis chapter 1). Yet they recognized in their daily existence that people suffer from evil (Sirach 40:1-5). They believed Yahweh causes everything and felt that he must likewise cause suffering (Amos 3:6; Proverbs 16:4).

The Hebrews' enslavement in Egypt was their touchstone of historical suffering. It became a pattern for them, because Yahweh's saving action in the Exodus was their clearest participation in his love and protection (Numbers 20:15-16). Israel also believed that Yahweh used suffering to convert his people — to remind them of their dependence upon him alone (Leviticus 26:40-45; Deuteronomy 4:30-31). Psalm 16 sings of Israel's total dependence on Yahweh: "You are my Lord, apart from you I have no good." Any other good was meager and inadequate to fulfill Israel's desires. Psalm 73:23-27 echoes the song: "Yet with you I shall always be; you have hold of my right hand; with your counsel you guide me, and in the end you will receive me in glory. Whom else have I in heaven? And when I am with you, the earth delights me not."

Even in their early history, Israel knew that suffering resulted from evil. It produced slavery and national oppression as well as individual pain. Nonetheless, Israel stood firm in the belief that Yahweh acted to relieve suffering, just as he had in the Exodus. In addition, however, they came to see that Yahweh also *judged* individuals according to their behavior, punishing the wicked and rewarding the just. They came to this conclusion from their reflection on Yahweh's nature (Jeremiah 32:19; Psalm 62:12; Job 34:11).

Suffering was considered a just retribution for sin (Numbers 12:1-15). Since the covenanted Israel was a community, they shared responsibility. The whole nation suffered if any of its members sinned (Joshua 7:1-11).

The prophets proclaimed that Israel's suffering could be attributed to its unfaithfulness to the covenant with Yahweh (Isaiah 3:13-26, 22:1-14; Jeremiah 2:19, 4:18). They saw the power of Yahweh at work in the foreign nations who conquered them (Isaiah 10:5-6). They believed Yahweh sent suffering not because he was mean, but because he wanted them to wake up to their own failures and evils. He was teaching them that evil produces evil.

Toward the end of the period in which the prophets lived, one of them began to see that suffering enabled Israel to atone for the sins of others. This theme is prominent in the songs about the Suffering Servant of the Lord (Isaiah 42:1-4, 49:1-7, 52:13-15, 53:1-2). Five hundred years later, the Jewish followers of Jesus would see these prophecies fulfilled in their Master. The point of the Suffering Servant songs is this: by his suffering this Servant substituted himself for people who otherwise would suffer. This suffering formed a unique relationship between the Servant and Yahweh (see especially Isaiah 53:12).

In exile in Babylon, Israelite prophets urged the people to reflect on their evil ways. This reflection bolstered their trust in their loving God. For the prophets insisted that God would restore them to their own home country and to freedom *in spite of* their sins.

In spite of the Hebrew conviction that Yahweh punished only the wicked, the Old Testament is full of examples of faithful ones who suffered. The suffering did not deter their devotion to Yahweh, however bitter it might be. Outstanding examples were Abraham, Joseph, Hosea, Daniel, Susanna, and especially Jeremiah. The examples of these and other more ordinary people led to the recognition that often the unjust seemed to be blessed while the just suffered. This problem was variously answered at different times in Old Testament development. It seems never to have been fully solved. But one thing did remain clear: whether they suffered or not, the just were not to abandon their vocation to holiness, their relationship with Yahweh.

The great teachers of Israel, called the Wisdom School, discussed the issue of suffering over and over. Though unclear as to why they had to suffer, these teachers believed that through suffering Israel's relationship with Yahweh would be strengthened. Sirach 2:4-6 urges: "Accept whatever befalls you, in crushing misfortune be patient; for in fire gold is tested, and worthy men in the crucible of humiliation. Trust God and he will help you; make straight your ways and hope in him."

The Book of Job is a dramatic discussion of suffering and evil in which several possible views are represented. Still the same point remains: even the suffering man need not weaken in his love and devotion to Yahweh. "The Lord gave and the Lord has taken away; blessed be the name of the Lord!" (Job 1:21) "We accept good things from God; and should we not accept evil?" (Job 2:10)

Suffering was thus seen in Old Testament thinking as a necessity brought on by unfaithfulness, though there was some conflict about this. (They often left the conflict unresolved in the mystery of Yahweh's power.) Yet suffering had a cleansing power. It humbled Yahweh's sinful people, converted and restored them to a sincere covenant relationship with him.

Scripture References

The Old Testament teaches that all suffer and that Yahweh involves himself in this human condition.
>Sirach 40:1-5
>Amos 3:6
>Proverbs 16:4

Israel suffered because of its unfaithfulness to Yahweh.
>Isaiah 3:13-26, 22:1-14
>Jeremiah 2:19, 4:18

Yahweh used suffering to move Israel to conversion.
>Leviticus 26:40-45
>Deuteronomy 4:30-31

For a more extended discussion of suffering, read the Book of Job in its entirety.
Isaiah prophesied about the Suffering Servant.
>Isaiah 42:1-14
>49:1-7
>52:13-15
>53:1-12

Suffering is a frequent theme of the Psalms.
>Psalms 13, 30, 37, 38, 62, 69, 73, 75,
>77, 78, 86, 107, 116, 140, 141

Discussion Questions

1. What was the purpose of suffering in the Old Testament?

2. What did the Exodus teach the Israelites about suffering?

3. How were suffering and faithfulness related to the covenant?

4. Why do the just suffer?

5. What significant idea about suffering is found in the Suffering Servant prophecies of Isaiah?

6. How do I react to hardships and suffering in my life?

7. Am I dependent on God when things go well? When life is painful? When am I most faithful to God?

Prayer Service

All: In the name of the Father and of the Son and of the Holy Spirit. Amen.

Leader: The only way to overcome suffering in life is to place our trust in the Lord God. He will always save us. Let us listen to the revelation spoken by the prophet Isaiah.

Reader: (Proclaims Isaiah 51:12-16.)

Leader: Let us meditate on these words for a few moments.

All: (Meditate in silence for a few moments.)

Leader: Let us respond by praying from Psalm 37.

All: In all our suffering, we trust in the Lord, our Savior.

Leader: Do not worry about the wicked, do not envy those who do wrong. Quick as the grass they wither, fading like the green in the field.

All: In all our suffering, we trust in the Lord, our Savior.

Leader: Trust in Yahweh and do what is good, make your home in the land and live in peace; make Yahweh your only joy and he will give you what your heart desires.

All: In all our suffering, we trust in the Lord, our Savior.

Leader: Commit your fate to Yahweh, trust in him and he will act: making your virtue clear as the light, your integrity as bright as noon.

All: In all our suffering, we trust in the Lord, our Savior.

Leader: Be quiet before Yahweh, and wait patiently for him, not worrying about men who make their fortunes, about men who scheme to bring the poor and needy down.

All: In all our suffering, we trust in the Lord, our Savior.

Leader: Enough of anger, leave rage aside, do not worry, nothing but evil can come of it: for the wicked will be expelled, while those who hope in Yahweh shall have the land for their own.

All: In all our suffering, we trust in the Lord, our Savior.

Leader: A little longer, and the wicked will be no more, search his place well, he will not be there; but the humble shall have the land for their own to enjoy untroubled peace.

All: In all our suffering, we trust in the Lord, our Savior.

Leader: Let us pray together:

All: Lord God, our Father, we thank you that our trust can always be in your strength. When we are hardpressed with suffering may we always turn to you and find in you the power to live and be strengthened. We pray in the name of Jesus. Amen.

14
Suffering in the New Testament

Background

Jesus suffered precisely because he was human. He experienced the human condition completely in all things, save sin. He saves us through this deep sharing in our common experience.

Suffering did not break Jesus, for his Father's Spirit was with him. He relied on this power alone. Our Lord promises us the same power, so we too can overcome evil and suffering. Paradoxically, he teaches that we conquer the effects of suffering and evil by relying on the Holy Spirit and giving in to the suffering that life bestows upon us.

Jesus was the model of the suffering one. He did not, however, dignify evil and suffering. It had no power over him. He accepted the suffering and thus broke its hold (1 Peter 2:18-24). Jesus did not look for pain or pleasure. Life gave him both. He lived each moment to its fullness regardless of what that moment was. Life brings us these same moments of joy and sorrow. We need only accept life as Jesus did and we will be empowered to profit from each moment.

Jesus suffered, but not because of any personal sinfulness. He suffered for a purpose: by enduring suffering while responding with love and faithfulness to his Father's will, he redeemed humankind from the effects of evil and suffering. Thus he demonstrated the essential strength of Christianity. Suffering on behalf of others relieves them from the affliction of evil. This revolutionary paradox is spelled out in Matthew 16:24-28.

For Jesus, suffering was a way to remember that it was by his Father's power that he lived. Things of this world could never bring fullness of life. His words of agony in the Garden reflected his total acceptance of his Father's plan: "Not my will but yours be done" (Luke 22:42). Jesus knew that if he was in total union with his Father's will, he would find the fulfillment of his life. For all this, he was glorified by his Father. All his followers who joined in his suffering were united in his glorification.

At the Last Supper, Jesus established the new covenant by which everyone could participate in his suffering and death, and likewise in the renewal of life through the Resurrection. He took upon himself the suffering of all, that all might have life without the effects of evil. As Luke 22:20 recounts: "He did the same with the cup after eating, saying as he did so: 'This cup is the new covenant in my blood, which will be shed for you.'"

Jesus did not enjoy suffering. He did not see any merit in it of itself. In fact he was distressed by it, prayed that it might pass away (Luke 22:41-44). Yet he accepted it voluntarily out of love for others (John 15:13). His early community, accordingly, interpreted Jesus' healings as signs that he was taking on the sufferings of others and redeeming them (Matthew 8:16-17).

Suffering by itself does not heal or save. Alone, it is simply grueling and stupid. But Jesus' suffering had meaning because his intention was to lay down his life for his friends. Thus Jesus fulfilled the prophecies of Isaiah as the Suffering Servant who brought redemption to his people (Matthew 12:17-21; Acts 2:23-24, 3:13, 4:10-12; 1 John 2:2, 4:10).

The followers of Jesus were reminded that they would not be greater than their Master. Therefore, they could expect suffering and persecution (Matthew 10:24; John 15:18-21). To follow the Christ one had to deny oneself and take up one's cross (Matthew 16:24; Mark 8:34-35; Luke 9:23). The New Testament teaches further that one must learn to suffer injustices and evil with joy, for Jesus' sake (1 Peter 4:15-16; James 1:2; 2 Corinthians 4:9-11).

Paul, learning from experience, reflected that in weakness we actually become strong. We become strong because our suffering moves us to depend upon God, whose power overcomes evil and its consequences (2 Corinthians 12:9-10). Paul also shows that suffering benefits not only the individual but the entire Mystical Body of Christ. He rejoiced in his suffering for its benefit to the early Christian community (2 Corinthians 2:3-7).

The Letter to the Hebrews knows the value of Jesus' suffering. It places it in the rich context of Jewish tradition. Jesus, as the high priest, sacrificed himself and was the victim representing all humankind once and for all (Hebrews 2:9, 7:27, 9:24-28).

The eternal value of the Lord's suffering was a basic tenet of the instructions given to prospective converts in the early community. Via Isaiah's prophecy, Phillip proclaims to the Ethiopian court official that this is the "good news of Jesus" (Acts 8:26-35).

The early community of Jesus was often reminded that its suffering was not the end of their world. Suffering had no ultimate power over them. They believed that by submitting to suffering and death, Jesus had conquered these realities. All they needed to do was walk in the Master's footsteps, with his point of view. "Bow humbly under God's mighty hand, so that in due time he may lift you high. Cast all your cares on him because he cares for you" (1 Peter 5:6-7).

In Stephen's speech of self-defense before the Jewish leaders, he reviewed Israel's history and sufferings. He spoke of how the God of Israel had always saved his people. He reminded them that Yahweh had sent prophets to warn them, prophets who had always been persecuted. Concluding, Stephen accused the Jewish leaders of Jesus' murder. Angry at his words, the leaders condemned him to death. Stephen died echoing his Master's viewpoint: "As Stephen was being stoned he could be heard praying, 'Lord Jesus, receive my spirit.' He fell to his knees and cried out in a loud voice, 'Lord, do not hold this sin against them' " (Acts 7, especially verses 59-60).

Jesus suffered so that he could be joined to us. Because he loved people, he laid down his life day after day. The result was redemption. He calls us to do the same for the same reason!

Scripture References

Jesus accepted suffering, breaking its hold on humanity.
>1 Peter 2:18-24

The revolutionary paradox of the concept of Christian suffering!
>Matthew 16:24-28

Jesus fulfilled the "Suffering Servant" prophecies of Isaiah.
>Matthew 12:17-21
>Acts 2:23-24, 3:13, 4:10-12
>1 John 2:2, 4:10

Jesus accepted suffering out of love for others.
>Galatians 2:20
>John 15:13

To take up one's cross is to follow the risen Lord.
>Matthew 16:24
>Mark 8:34-35
>Luke 9:23

In the weakness of suffering, we become strong.
>2 Corinthians 12:9-10

Suffering not only strengthens the individual but the whole community of Christ.
>2 Corinthians 2:3-7

Discussion Questions

1. Why did Jesus suffer? Why do I suffer?

2. How was Jesus' suffering redemptive? Is mine? How?

3. What is the revolutionary teaching of Christianity about suffering? What does it mean to take up one's cross?

4. What is the significance of the Eucharist in the theme of suffering?

5. What did Jesus overcome by suffering?

6. What experiences of suffering have I had that turned out to be strengthening experiences?

7. How does one "give in" to suffering without being destroyed?

8. Why does modern American society attempt to avoid any form of suffering?

Prayer Service

All: In the name of the Father and of the Son and of the Holy Spirit. Amen.

Leader: Jesus' suffering gives us the example to suffer patiently that greater good can come. Let us listen to the First Letter of Peter.

Reader: *(Proclaims 1 Peter 2:19-24.)*

Leader: Let us meditate on these sacred words.

All: *(Meditate in silence for a few moments.)*

Leader: Let us respond by praying from Psalm 107.

All: The Lord heals us in suffering.

Leader: Give thanks to Yahweh, for he is good, his love is everlasting: let these be the words of Yahweh's redeemed, those he has redeemed from the oppressor's clutches, by bringing them home from foreign countries, from east and west, from north and south.

All: The Lord heals us in suffering.

Leader: Some had lost their way in the wilds and the desert, not knowing how to reach an inhabited town; they were hungry and desperately thirsty, their courage was running low.

All: The Lord heals us in suffering.

Leader: Then they called to Yahweh in their trouble and he rescued them from their sufferings, guiding them by a route leading direct to an inhabited town.

All: The Lord heals us in suffering.

Leader: Let these thank Yahweh for his love, for his marvels on behalf of men; satisfying the hungry, he fills the starving with good things.

All: The Lord heals us in suffering.

Leader: Let us pray together:

All: Lord Jesus, we are empowered by your Spirit to conquer our sufferings. We follow your example and turn to you for strength. In our sufferings may we patiently endure and participate in your redeeming love for all the world. Amen.

15
Discipleship in the Old Testament

Background

Discipleship was not a common term for Old Testament authors. In Isaiah 8:16-20, the followers of the prophet Isaiah are called "disciples" whose duty it is to keep his words so that when the time comes, they can instruct others. If "discipleship" and "faithful following" mean the same thing, we can learn from investigating the Old Testament concept of the "faithful remnant." This remnant tradition was to be eventually fulfilled in the person of Jesus and his disciples.

The basic sequence in the remnant tradition followed a pattern: Israel ignored Yahweh and committed apostasy; then it was destroyed. The destruction was a purification of Israel, from which a faithful remnant remained. This remnant was always a very small portion of the people — a portion who had remained faithful to the covenant. The existence of the remnant assured the future of the descendants of Abraham. The Jews never believed that destruction would not be followed by Yahweh's merciful restoration of his people. The remnant was a sign of Yahweh's mercy and saving power as well as a sign of Israel's failure toward the covenant.

Several times in the early Old Testament, we find a faithful remnant remaining: after the flood (Genesis 6:5-8, 7:1, 23); after the destruction of Sodom (Genesis 18:17-33, 19:29). Here the remnant is Lot and his family, saved because of Abraham's faithfulness to Yahweh. Then there is Joseph's acceptance of his brothers when their destruction was threatened, which assured a remnant from among the descendants God had promised to their father Abraham (Genesis 45:7). This theme of the faithful few sustaining the promises to the chosen people is also seen in the reduction of Gideon's forces to 300 men (Judges 7:1-8). In the story of Elijah, the remnant is to be all who have not worshiped pagan gods (1 Kings 19:18).

As time went on and unfaithfulness persisted, two opposing views arose about whether a remnant would remain at all. Some passages predict that there will be no community of faithful after the destruction (Jeremiah 50:26 and some of Ezekiel). These passages were strong in their denial of a remnant because Israel's evil seemed so total that total destruction seemed inevitable to these prophets. However, other passages retain the expectation of a remnant.

In his attempt to wake Israel up, the prophet Amos attacked the notion that the people of Israel could continue to alienate themselves from Yahweh and still retain the presumptuous hope of a future remnant (Amos 3:12, 5:3, 6:9, 9:1). Amos taught that Israel was so corrupt that if a remnant survived, it would depend wholly on Israel's about-face and Yahweh's free act of mercy (Amos 5:6). Yahweh "may" have pity on the remnant if they "seek good, not evil" and "let justice prevail" (Amos 5:14-15).

Isaiah 17:6 treats the idea of a remnant as a threat from Yahweh. The threat is that *only* a remnant will remain if Israel does not return to the covenant. Although God had promised Abraham that his descendants would outnumber the sands of the sea, Isaiah says that Israel's unfaithfulness will reduce these numbers to a faithful few (Isaiah 10:20-22). Isaiah calls for conversion and fidelity if there is to be any remnant at all. Even the remnant will be the "afflicted ones." The great prophet saw that the remnant would be the faithful Jews living outside of Israel itself, after the destruction had come (Isaiah 11:16).

A contemporary of Isaiah, Micah predicts a remnant: "I will make of the lame a remnant, and of those driven far off a strong nation; and the Lord shall be king over them on Mount Zion, from now on forever" (Micah 4:7).

Jeremiah 11:9 saw that Israel had entered into a conspiracy against Yahweh. Israel would be totally destroyed with only a faithful few remaining. Even this remnant would suffer greatly due to the wholesale unfaithfulness of Israel (Jeremiah 8:3).

Zephaniah 2:3 calls to the faithful few: "Seek the Lord, all you humble of the earth, who have observed his law; seek justice, seek humility; *perhaps* you may be sheltered on the day of the Lord's anger." He predicts that only a few will be protected: "But I will leave as a remnant in your midst a people humble and lowly, who shall take refuge in the name of the Lord: the remnant of Israel. They shall do no wrong and speak no lies; nor shall there be found in their mouths a deceitful tongue; they shall pasture and couch their flocks with none to disturb them" (3:12-13).

After the Exile in Babylon, the consequences of unfaithfulness now fulfilled, Zechariah 8:11-13 teaches that the remnant left surviving will be the ultimate blessing for unfaithful Israel: "But now I will not deal with the remnant of this people as in former days, says the Lord of hosts, for it is the seedtime of peace . . . . Just as you were a curse among the nations, O house of Judah and house of Israel, so will I save you that you may be a blessing; do not fear, but let your hands be strong." Thus at this time, the theme of the remnant came to refer to the community that existed in Jerusalem after their return from Exile (Haggai 1:12-14, 2:2; Ezra 9:8; Nehemiah 1:2-3). The remnant would become a spiritual reality, distinct from Israel as a political reality — although Israel herself did not recognize this for at least another 500 years.

Yahweh promised that he would gather the faithful remnant from their scattered homes among the nations and unite them in the land of their ancestors (Isaiah 11:11; Micah 2:12). This, of course, implied for the Jews a political reality — and the conflict still is not settled over what Yahweh really meant.

The prophecies about the remnant actually were fulfilled again later. Even after the destruction of the second temple in 70 A.D., a remnant of the chosen people remained. They became a sign to the world of the faithfulness and saving power of Yahweh.

However, the early Christian community believed that the true remnant was the person of Jesus extended in his faithful disciples. These faithful ones united with Jesus in perfect humility and obedience to the divine plan of the Father (1 Peter 2:18-25; Revelation 12:17).

Paul writes to the Romans (11:1-12) about the remnant. He teaches that through Jesus the Gentiles have been joined to the faithful remnant of Israel. However, in the mind of Paul, the remnant consisted only in the small number of Jews who had believed in Jesus and thus became part of the new Israel of Jesus and his community (Romans 9:25-29, 11:1-7).

The covenant called upon Israel to be faithful. History would show that only a few remained faithful. Yet Yahweh would accept the faithfulness of the "remnant" few. As the body of his Son, Jesus, the remnant would be the sacrament of salvation for all the world.

Scripture References

The remnant of Israel consisted of those who remained faithful and survived the Babylonian Exile.
Haggai 1:12-14, 2:2
Ezra 9:8
Nehemiah 1:2-3

Early Old Testament understandings of "remnant."
Genesis 6:5-8, 7:1, 23, 18:17-33, 19:15-29, 45:7
Judges 7:1-7

Amos warned against hoping for the remnant while remaining unfaithful.
Amos 3:12, 5:3-6, 6:9

Yahweh promised he would gather the remnant as a blessing for Israel.
    Isaiah 11:11
    Micah 2:12

Paul taught that the remnant of Israel was incorporated into the body of the risen Lord.
    Romans 9:25-29, 11:1-12

Discussion Questions

1. Why did Israel end up only being a remnant?

2. Why did some of the prophets predict there would not be a remnant?

3. Why did Israel enter into a "conspiracy" against Yahweh?

4. What characteristics are found in the people of the remnant?

5. How has the Lord shown me in my life that he hasn't rejected me in spite of my unfaithfulness?

6. Why is it difficult for us in our modern society to be faithful to the Lord?

Prayer Service

All: In the name of the Father and of the Son and of the Holy Spirit. Amen.

Leader: In spite of unfaithfulness, Yahweh promised his people that the faithful remnant would be the cause of his blessing. Let us listen to the comforting promise as proclaimed by Yahweh through the prophet Zechariah, after the Exile was over.

Reader: *(Proclaims Zechariah 8:1-8.)*

Leader: Let us reflect on these words of the prophet.

All: *(Meditate in silence for a few moments.)*

Leader: Let us respond by praying Psalm 85.

All: The mercy of the Lord has restored his people.

Leader: Yahweh, you favor your own country, you bring back the captives of Jacob, you take your people's guilt away, you blot out all their sins, you retract all your anger, you abjure your fiery rage.

All: The mercy of the Lord has restored his people.

Leader: Bring us back, God our savior, master your resentment against us. Do you mean to be angry with us forever, to prolong your wrath age after age? Will you not give us life again, for your people to rejoice in you? Yahweh, show us your love, grant us your saving help.

All: The mercy of the Lord has restored his people.

Leader: I am listening. What is Yahweh saying? What God is saying means peace for his people, for his friends, if only they renounce their folly; for those who fear him, his saving help is near, and the glory will then live in our country.

All: The mercy of the Lord has restored his people.

Leader: Love and Loyalty now meet, Righteousness and Peace now embrace; Loyalty reaches up from earth and Righteousness leans down from heaven. Yahweh himself bestows happiness as our soil gives its harvest, Righteousness always preceding him and Peace following his footsteps.

All: The mercy of the Lord has restored his people.

Leader: Let us pray together:

All: Lord God, our Father, we thank you for your kindness in restoring us to your loving affection for us. We pray that we may always have the courage to live according to your covenant with us and proclaim you as our God and live as your people. We pray in Jesus' name. Amen.

16
Discipleship in the New Testament

Background

In Jesus' time, the rabbis had disciples. Most rabbis belonged to the sect or party known as Pharisees and were experts in religious law. Their disciples studied the law under their instruction and would in time become rabbis themselves.

Jesus was called "rabbi." Yet his disciples were distinctly different from other rabbinical disciples. They did not concern themselves with learning the law but with experiencing the person of Jesus and his teachings. They also knew that they would not become equal to their Master, but would always be his witnesses. They transmitted the personality and power of the "Rabbi" Jesus.

In the New Testament, the word *disciple* has several meanings. In Philippians 4:11 and 1 Timothy 5:4, it means a learner. In Mark 2:14 and Mark 10:21, it means a follower. In the Gospels, disciples "follow Jesus" and share in his human condition, good and bad.

Jesus chose his first disciples personally. They were called "The Twelve" and were empowered by their Master to have authority in expelling demons, curing sickness, and preaching the message of their Master (Matthew 10:1-4). The disciples were to remain loyal (John 6:66), be servants to others in their need (Mark 9:33-35), be totally devoted to the person of Jesus (Luke 14:25-27). Later, they were to shepherd the flock (Acts 20:27-31).

Jesus asked his disciples to renounce everything but him, to accept him as the master of their lives and to look upon all reality from his perspective (Luke 9:57-62, 14:23-34).

The Lord teaches that only by remaining intimately united with him does the disciple have any power. "I am the vine, you are the branches. He who lives in me and I in him, will produce abundantly, for apart from me you can do nothing" (John 15:5). Discipleship is a call to holiness, to imitation of Jesus, the Holy One (1 Peter 2:1-10). Yet the Lord empowered his disciples to accomplish the same signs and wonders that he had during his time among them. Thus glory would be continuously given to the Father (John 14:12-13; Acts 5:12). The continuing intimacy required for this is provided to his faithful ones in the bread of the Eucharist, which brings eternal life (John 6:47-51).

Jesus warned his disciples — and us today — that riches could lure them away from loyalty to him and service to others. Riches produce a self-reliant attitude which does not match the vocation to dependency on the Lord and openness to others' needs (1 Timothy 6:10; Matthew 13:22).

The Lord promised beautiful things to those who would be his disciples and live his way. We read some of them in John 15:9-17.

The disciples of Jesus are assured that they need not worry about life. Loyalty and fidelity to the Lord's way will bring us his protection and all the things that we need to be fulfilled (Matthew 6:25-34).

Throughout the New Testament we find characteristics of a disciple. We need to find our security in the Lord (Philippians 4:11), serve those closest to us (1 Timothy 5:4), and depend in humility on the Lord (Matthew 11:29). Chapter 25 of Matthew reflects some stances of a disciple: waiting for the Lord, exercising the talents the Lord has given, serving the least of the Lord's brothers and sisters. The most important attitude of a true disciple of Jesus is love. Paul reminds the community that without this basic attitude of love, there is nothing (1 Corinthians 13). Jesus wanted his disciples to bear others' burdens and serve others in love as he did (Matthew 9:9-13; Mark 8:34-38, 10:32-45).

Paul points out that the Spirit moves in the lives of the Lord's followers. True disciples give thanks for everything in the name of the Lord (Ephesians 5:20). They do everything for the honor of the Lord rather than for the praise of men (Colossians 3:23-24). The fruit of the Spirit can be seen in the disciples' attitudes of love, joy, peace, patient endurance, kindness, generosity, faith, mildness, and chastity (Galatians 5:22-23).

Jesus is united forever with all of his disciples, his faithful followers. Paul explains this to the Romans by saying that we are all members of the one body, Jesus, with different gifts to serve each other in the community (Romans 12:3-8).

The earliest Christian community of disciples followed the Lord by praying together, sharing all things in common, and serving one another's needs (Acts 2:42-47, 4:32-35). The early Christians were certain that they could place their confidence in God for all their needs (1 John 5:14-15).

To follow Jesus is to come to him, to listen to his word and put it into practice. It is to be attached to his person and his message. It is to love him and proclaim his saving power in our lives to others. It is to renounce ourselves, carry our crosses patiently and joyously, and depend totally upon his power and love. The result of such devotion is peace in our hearts and eternal glory with Jesus in the eternal kingdom of his Father and the Spirit.

Scripture References

Various meanings of the concept of disciple.
> Philippians 4:11
> 1 Timothy 5:4
> Mark 2:14 and Mark 10:21

Disciples are called to be ambassadors and reconcilers.
> 2 Corinthians 5:18-21

Jesus' teachings about discipleship.
> Matthew 5-7

Characteristics of a true disciple.
> Matthew 9:9-13, 11:29, Chapter 25
> Mark 8:34-38, 10:32-45
> 1 Corinthians 13
> Galatians 5:22-23
> Ephesians 5:20
> Colossians 3:23-24

The Lord calls on his disciples to renounce everything that would prevent absolute loyalty to him.
> Luke 9:57-62, 14:23-34

At the Last Supper, as told in John's Gospel, Jesus expressed his feelings about his disciples and his promises to them.
> John, Chapters 14-17

In the Eucharist, the Lord is intimately united with his faithful ones.
> John 6:45-51

The pattern of life in the early Christian community reflected their discipleship.
> Acts 2:42-47, 4:32-35

Discussion Questions

1. What are some of the basic characteristics of a disciple?

2. What mission does Jesus give to his disciples?

3. What promises does the Lord make to those who follow him faithfully?

4. What were the characteristics of the early Christian community?

5. Who is the Lord to me personally, and why do I feel called to be his disciple?

6. Why does Jesus ask me to renounce all things in order to follow him?

7. How can I proclaim the Good News in my daily life?

8. What do I need to do to get personally healthy with the Lord?

Prayer Service

All: In the name of the Father and of the Son and of the Holy Spirit. Amen.

Leader: Through the merciful love of the Lord, we are called to be his disciples, living stones of the living temple, Jesus. We are to proclaim the glorious works of the Lord. Let us listen to the words of Peter the apostle.

Reader: *(Proclaims 1 Peter 2:1-10.)*

Leader: Let us reflect on these words and their meaning in our lives.

All: *(Meditate in silence for a few moments.)*

Leader: Let us respond in prayer from John 17.

All: We give glory to the Lord by being his disciples.

Leader: I pray for them; I am not praying for the world but for those you have given me, because they belong to you: all I have is yours and all you have is mine, and in them I am glorified.

All: We give glory to the Lord by being his disciples.

Leader: I am not in the world any longer, but they are in the world, and I am coming to you. Holy Father, keep those you have given me true to your name, so that they may be one like us.

All: We give glory to the Lord by being his disciples.

Leader: While I was with them, I kept those you had given me true to your name. I have watched over them and not one is lost except the one who chose to be lost, and this was to fulfill the Scriptures.

But now I am coming to you and while still in the world I say these things to share my joy with them to the full.

All: We give glory to the Lord by being his disciples.

Leader: I passed your word on to them, and the world hated them, because they belong to the world no more than I belong to the world.

I am not asking you to remove them from the world, but to protect them from the evil one. They do not belong to the world any more than I belong to the world.

All: We give glory to the Lord by being his disciples.

Leader: Consecrate them in the truth; your word is truth. As you sent me into the world, I have sent them into the world, and for their sake I consecrate myself so that they too may be consecrated in truth.

All: We give glory to the Lord by being his disciples.

Leader: Let us pray together:

All: Lord Jesus, we thank you for calling us to be your faithful community of disciples. Empowered by your Spirit and filled with your love, we pledge to live our lives as living examples and witnesses to your power and glory. May the world come to know you and may we be your messengers all the days of our lives as we give you glory and praise forever and ever. Amen.